YAHYA IBRAHIM

Published by:

23-2 Jalan PJS 5/30, Petaling Jaya Commercial City
46150 Petaling Jaya, Selangor, Malaysia
+603-7772-3156 (office) / +6017-399-7411 (mobile)
info@tertib.press
www.tertib.press
@tertibpress (Facebook & Instagram)

Author	:	Yahya Ibrahim
Editor	:	Norashikin Azizan
Cover designer	:	Abdul Adzim Md Daim
Typesetter	:	Abdul Adzim Md Daim

RAMADAN THERAPY

First Edition: April 2022

Perpustakaan Negara Malaysia   Cataloguing-in-Publication Data

Yahya Ibrahim
رمضان = Ramadan Therapy / Yahya Ibrahim.
ISBN 978-967-2844-12-9
1. Ramadan.
2. Islam--Customs and practices.
3. Islam--Prayers and devotions.
4. Muslims--Conduct of life.
5. Religious life--Islam.
I. Title.
297.362

Contents

Foreword

Ramadan is the month of therapy and closure. It is a month of re-establishment of an individual's life after a year of ups and downs in faith. This is the month of obtaining hope and to becoming better out of it. May Allah grant the mercy to remain consistent in making these *du'ā'* during and after Ramadan as among the forms of daily therapy.

Tertib Publishing | tertib.press

Preface

Assalamualaikum warahmatullahi wabarakatuh. All praises be to Allah, the Lord of mankind. We send blessings and salutations upon Prophet Muhammad s.a.w., his family, his companions and those that are dear to him.

My aim over the next 29 or 30 days of Ramadan, is that we will study *duʿāʾ* of the Prophet Muhammad s.a.w., which can either be a verse of the Qur'an or something that he would be inspired by Allah s.w.t. to invoke Him through. These *duʿāʾ* are meant to be our Ramadan Therapy. All of us enter the month of Ramadan with pain. All of us enter it with something that is missing—there is either financial constraint or a health worry, for example. There may be something that keeps us up late at night with regard to our children or our loved ones.

For every believer, there must be something that keeps him awake, that gives him a 'headache'—we can never escape from it. May Allah s.w.t. give us those regular small headaches, rather than the major pain that is inflicted upon those who have strayed from the path of truth and guidance of our Prophet Muhammad s.a.w. Our hope *insha Allah*, is that we are going to learn 30 *du'ā'* that we can ponder, reflect upon, and more importantly, learn to apply.

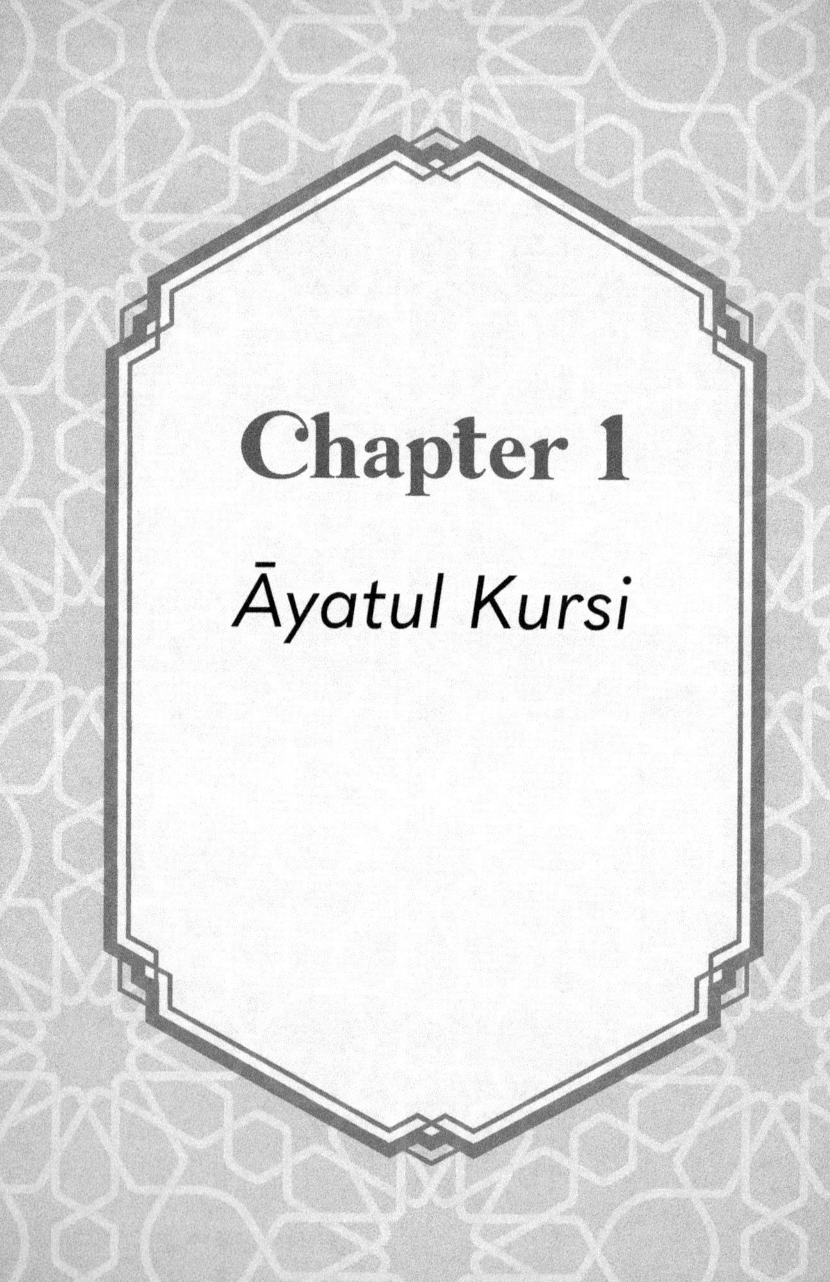

Chapter 1

Āyatul Kursi

ٱللَّهُ لَآ إِلَٰهَ إِلَّا هُوَ ٱلْحَىُّ ٱلْقَيُّومُ ۚ لَا تَأْخُذُهُۥ سِنَةٌ وَلَا نَوْمٌ ۚ لَّهُۥ مَا فِى ٱلسَّمَٰوَٰتِ وَمَا فِى ٱلْأَرْضِ ۗ مَن ذَا ٱلَّذِى يَشْفَعُ عِندَهُۥٓ إِلَّا بِإِذْنِهِۦ ۚ يَعْلَمُ مَا بَيْنَ أَيْدِيهِمْ وَمَا خَلْفَهُمْ ۖ وَلَا يُحِيطُونَ بِشَىْءٍ مِّنْ عِلْمِهِۦٓ إِلَّا بِمَا شَآءَ ۚ وَسِعَ كُرْسِيُّهُ ٱلسَّمَٰوَٰتِ وَٱلْأَرْضَ ۖ وَلَا يَـُٔودُهُۥ حِفْظُهُمَا ۚ وَهُوَ ٱلْعَلِىُّ ٱلْعَظِيمُ (٢٥٥)

Allahu lā ilāha illa huwal ḥaiyyul qayyum; la ta'khuzuhū sinatun wa lā nawm; lahū mā fissamāwāti wa mā fil a'rḍ; man dhalladhi yashfa'u 'indahū illā bi idhnih; ya'lamu mā bayna aydīhim wa mā khalfahum; wa lā yuḥīṭuna bishay i'mmin 'ilmihī illā bimā shāa'; wasi'a kursiyyuhus samā wāti wal arḍa wa lā ya ū'duhū ḥifẓuhumā; wa huwal 'aliyyul 'azeem.

Allah: There is no god but He, the Living, the All-Sustaining. Neither dozing nor sleep overtakes Him. To Him belongs all that is in the Heavens and all that is on the Earth. Who can intercede with Him without His permission? He knows what is before them and what is behind them; while they encompass nothing of His knowledge, except what He wills. His Kursi (Chair) extends to the Heavens and to the Earth, and it does not weary Him to look after them. He is the All-High, the Supreme. (255) (Surah al-Baqarah: Verse 255)

◆

The first *du'ā'* comes from the authentic *hadith* of the Prophet Muhammad s.a.w., Sahih Bukhari and Sahih Muslim; there are narrations about the virtue of this *āyat*. This magnificent *Āyatul Kursi* refers to the *Kursi* of *Ar-Rahman* and *Ar-Rahim* s.w.t. Now first, let us know its virtue. The Prophet s.a.w. said,

"It is the greatest verse in the Qur'an." (Sahih Muslim 810)

This is because it is a verse that is revealed to tell us about who Allah is. In fact, the very first word of *Āyatul Kursi* is, Allah.

ٱللَّهُ لَآ إِلَـٰهَ إِلَّا هُوَ ٱلْحَىُّ ٱلْقَيُّومُ

Second, it contains what is referred to by many of the *ulamā'*—Allah's greatest combination of names that is put together in our request of Him. In a *hadith* of Abu Umamah r.a., he said that the Prophet s.a.w. said,

"There are three *surah* that if you recite them, any one

of them, they contain Allah's greatest names." (Sunan Ibn Majah 3856)

Therefore, Abu Umamah r.a. said, "I looked into the three *surah* that the Prophet s.a.w. mentioned. Surah al-Baqarah, Surah Ali-Imran and Surah Ta-ha. I found that the only thing that those three *surah* had that were not found in other *surah* are the names of Allah, *al-Hayy* and *al-Qayyum*." In Surah al-Baqarah, these names of Allah—*al-Hayy* and *al-Qayyum* are found in *Āyatul Kursi*.

In Surah Ali-Imran, it begins, *bismillahirrahmanirrahim,*

$$الٓمّ (١) ٱللَّهُ لَآ إِلَـٰهَ إِلَّا هُوَ ٱلْحَىُّ ٱلْقَيُّومُ (٢)$$

(Ali-Imraan, 3:1-2)

In Surah Ta-Ha, Allah s.w.t. says,

$$وَعَنَتِ ٱلْوُجُوهُ لِلْحَىِّ ٱلْقَيُّومِ ۖ وَقَدْ خَابَ مَنْ حَمَلَ ظُلْمًا (١١١)$$

(Ta-Ha, 20:111)

In a *hadith* of Abu Hurairah r.a., in Sahih Bukhari, he related that he was visited by someone who taught him a certain thing, and the Prophet concurred that it was a correct teaching—even though the one who spoke to Abu Hurairah was one usually who deceived and misled.

The Prophet s.a.w. agreed that for the person who recites *Āyatul Kursi* in the evening, an angel stands at his guard, protecting him until the morning. And for the one who reads it in the morning, an angel stands at his guard until nighttime falls. (Sahih Bukhari 3275)

In an authentic *hadith*, the Prophet s.a.w. said,

"There is no home where *Āyatul Kursi* is recited in it, and that the *shaytān* does have a place or an abode to live in." (Sahih Muslim 2018)

They flee from the recitation of *Āyatul Kursi* and from the recitation of Surah al-Baqarah. In fact, many of our *ʿulamā'* say that the preference of reciting Surah al-Baqarah is because of *Āyatul Kursi* being in it. *Āyatul Kursi* is the verse that tells us best about Allah s.w.t. There is none that we worship, other than He.

Therefore, let us mechanise this. We have understood that it is a healing, that it was used as a medicine by the Prophet s.a.w. and the *ṣaḥābah*. It is a protection against the seen and the unseen forces. In an authentic *hadith* of Abu Dharr r.a., Prophet s.a.w. said,

"Let yourself be protected from the devils of humankind, as well as the unseen nefarious *Jinn* forces." The Prophet s.a.w. then prescribed to him (Abu Dharr) *Āyatul Kursi* to be recited in his evenings and mornings. (Sunan At-Tirmidhi 2144)

Let us rephrase the ways to use it. First, the moment we wake up and have made the mention of Allah, made the *dhikr* of Allah, made *wuḍū'* and made our *ṣolah*. Let our reading of *Āyatul Kursi* commence. The Prophet s.a.w. said in an authentic *hadith*,

"There is protection of those who reads *Āyatul Kursi*". That is because of the reading of *Āyatul Kursi*, after every one of our five compulsory prayers, that our place in Jannah is guaranteed. (Sunan Nasa'i 9848)

Thus, include them into our daily routine. *Āyatul Kursi* should be a part of our morning *adhkar*. What is the intention when we read these *adhkar*? Firstly, that Allah blesses us with nearness to Him through it, that we grow our love for Allah. Secondly, that Allah protects us as a result of our belief in Him s.w.t. And thirdly, that it is something that acts as a protection for our household, and those who will feel the radiating from us of its blessings and *barakah*.

As a flow, recite *Āyatul Kursi* in the morning. Then after every *ṣolah*. Next, at the moment of any fear. Fear of envy, fear of the evil eye, fear of illness, unwellness, or whatever it may be. Make sure that we recite *Āyatul Kursi* in these situations. Lastly, recite it before we sleep. The Prophet s.a.w. would recite it any time after *Solatul Maghrib*, but in particular when on his bed. As he sat in his bed, he would bring his hands together and he would recite Surah al-Fātihah. In another narration, he would recite the three Quls (Surah al-Ikhlās, Surah al-Falaq, Surah an-Nas), three times each, Surah al-Fātihah seven times, or he would recite the last two verses of Surah al-Baqarah and also recite *Āyatul Kursi.* Therefore, on our bed, in our place of retirement at the end of the day, practise this. Read *Āyatul Kursi* at night.

To recap what we have said, recite *Āyatul* Kursi after the five daily prayers, in the morning, in the evening, at any time when we feel something is not right or when we are feeling unwell. *Āyatul Kursi* can also be a medicine. What we would do is we would recite it as we cup our hands, breathe it into our hands and touch the part of our body that is hurting, just like when we have neck pain, we would touch our actual skin with it, asking Allah s.w.t. to heal us. These are among the spiritual remedies of the Prophet Muhammad s.a.w.

The Qur'an is also a healing for that of which is in the chest. When we believe the message of *Āyatul Kursi,* we come to understand that Allah s.w.t. is The One who never slumbers, never sleeps and is always awake. He is *al-Hayy.* His Existence is the reason for our existence. He is *al-Qayyum,* The One who is establishing everything that He has brought into existence. To Him belongs all that there is in the Heavens and the Earth—including ourselves and our problems and difficulties, nothing is beyond Him. No one can speak before Him, no one can change something in front of Him except that which He has ordered. No one can intercede on another's behalf. No one can change their own fate, except through Him.

Lastly, one of the reasons we recite it is to change our fate into something that will cure or heal us and all of them we ask from Allah s.w.t. We ask Allah s.w.t. to make us from those who are successful in this blessed month of Ramadan. We seek Allah in what is before us, what is behind us, what is to come to us. He knows our pain and our sorrow, and with Him is the cure and the healing. We ask Allah s.w.t. who holds dominion of the Heavens and the Earth, that His *Kursi* is greater than all of that is in the Heavens and the Earth. All of them are nothing but a ring within a ring, within the magnificent creation of Allah. We ask Allah s.w.t., with His knowledge and power to assist us in all that we are lacking in which we find difficult, and to bless us in our days and our nights, *Allahumma āmīn*.

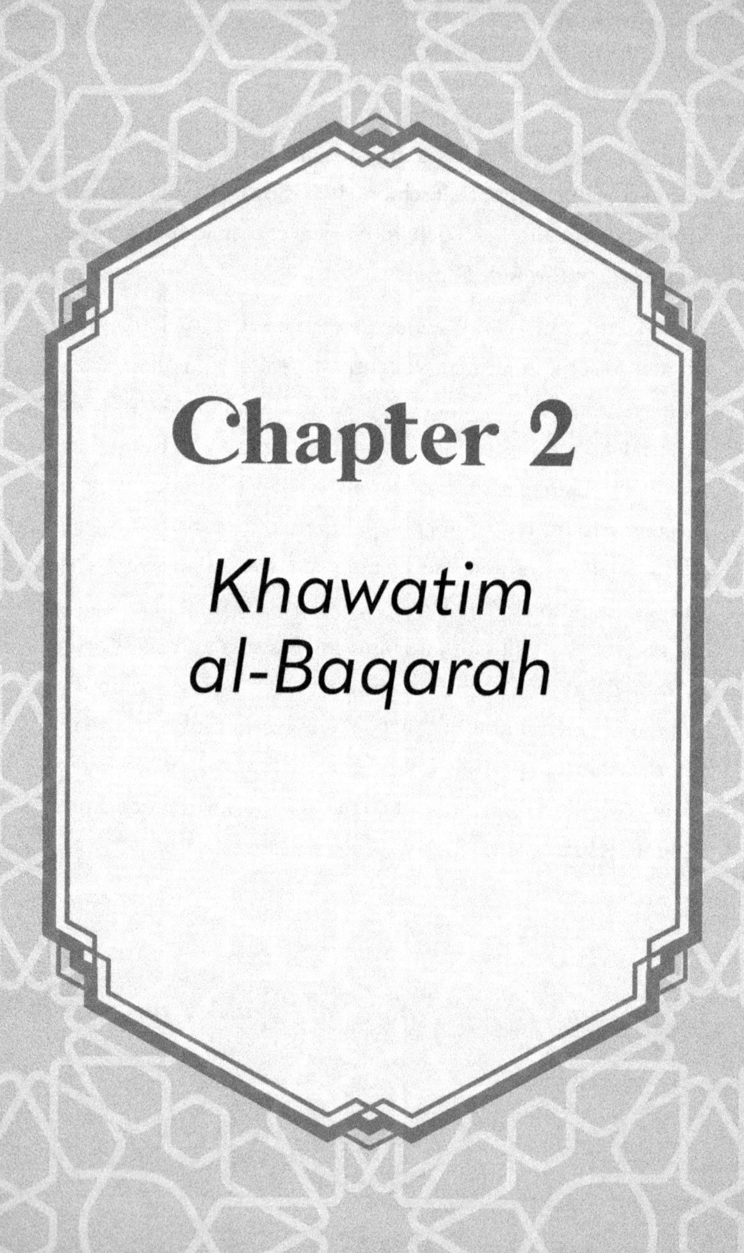
Chapter 2

Khawatim
al-Baqarah

ءَامَنَ ٱلرَّسُولُ بِمَآ أُنزِلَ إِلَيْهِ مِن رَّبِّهِۦ وَٱلْمُؤْمِنُونَ ۚ كُلٌّ ءَامَنَ بِٱللَّهِ وَمَلَـٰٓئِكَتِهِۦ وَكُتُبِهِۦ وَرُسُلِهِۦ لَا نُفَرِّقُ بَيْنَ أَحَدٍ مِّن رُّسُلِهِۦ ۚ وَقَالُوا۟ سَمِعْنَا وَأَطَعْنَا ۖ غُفْرَانَكَ رَبَّنَا وَإِلَيْكَ ٱلْمَصِيرُ (٢٨٥) لَا يُكَلِّفُ ٱللَّهُ نَفْسًا إِلَّا وُسْعَهَا ۚ لَهَا مَا كَسَبَتْ وَعَلَيْهَا مَا ٱكْتَسَبَتْ ۗ رَبَّنَا لَا تُؤَاخِذْنَآ إِن نَّسِينَآ أَوْ أَخْطَأْنَا ۚ رَبَّنَا وَلَا تَحْمِلْ عَلَيْنَآ إِصْرًا كَمَا حَمَلْتَهُۥ عَلَى ٱلَّذِينَ مِن قَبْلِنَا ۚ رَبَّنَا وَلَا تُحَمِّلْنَا مَا لَا طَاقَةَ لَنَا بِهِۦ ۖ وَٱعْفُ عَنَّا وَٱغْفِرْ لَنَا وَٱرْحَمْنَآ ۚ أَنتَ مَوْلَىٰنَا فَٱنصُرْنَا عَلَى ٱلْقَوْمِ ٱلْكَـٰفِرِينَ (٢٨٦)

Āmanar rasūlu bimā unzila ilayhi mir rabbihī wal mu'minūna kullun āmana billahi wamalā-ikatihī wakutubihī warusulihī lā nufarriqu bayna aḥadim mir rusulihi waqālū sam'inā wa aṭa'nā ghufrānaka rabbanā wa-ilayka almasīr (2:285)

Lā yukallifu Allahu nafsan illā wus'aha lahā mā kasabat wa 'uluyhā mak tasabat rabbanā lātu-akhidhnā in nasīnā aw akhṭa'na rabbanā walā taḥmil ʿalaynā iṣran kamā ḥamaltahū ʿala alladhīna min qablinā rabbanā walā tuḥammilnā mā lā ṭāqata lanā bihi wa'fu ʿannā waghfir lanā warḥamnā anta mawlānā fanṣurnā ʿalalqawmi alkāfirīn (2:286)

The Messenger has believed in what has been revealed to him from his Lord, and the believers as well. All have believed in Allah and His angels and His Books and His Messengers. "We make no division between any of His Messengers," and they have said: "We have listened and obeyed. Our Lord, (we seek) Your pardon! And to You is the return." (285) Allah does not obligate anyone beyond his capacity. For him is what he has earned, and on him that he has incurred. "Our Lord do not hold us accountable, if we forget or make a mistake, and, Our Lord, do not place on us such a burden as You have placed on those before us, and, Our Lord, do not make us bear a burden for which we have no strength. And pardon us, and grant us forgiveness, and have mercy on us. You are our Lord. So then help us against the disbelieving people." (286) (al-Baqarah, 2:285-286)

———— ◆ ————

The last two verses of Surah al-Baqarah are referred to as *Khawatim al-Baqarah*, the seal of the *surah*. Now, a little background—it is important to note that these two verses need to link with the verse that precedes them, which is verse 284, Allah s.w.t. says, "To Allah belongs what is in the Heavens and what is in the Earth. If you disclose what is in your hearts or conceal it, Allah shall hold you accountable for it, then He will forgive whom He wills and punish whom He wills. Allah is powerful over everything. (284)"

The moment this verse was revealed, the *ṣaḥābah* r.a. panicked. The companions said, "O' Rasulullah, this verse has come to you with something that we cannot withstand. Allah is going to hold me accountable to my thoughts or is it my actions?" The Messenger of Allah s.a.w. then received a new revelation from Allah s.w.t. to quell their fear and their angst. In that new revelation are these two verses that we are about to study. The Prophet s.a.w. said that an important benefit and virtue of these two verses is that they will suffice anyone of their needs. Therefore, if there is any need that we have—be it physical, emotional, health and financial—reciting and maintaining these two verses shall suffice that need in our belief that Allah hears us invoking Him.

In addition, the Prophet s.a.w. said, "I was given from the treasure of the "*Arsh* of Ar-Rahman"—meaning from the Gardens of Jannah beneath the Magnificent Throne

(*'Arsh*), and he was referring to these last two verses of Surah al-Baqarah. The Prophet s.a.w. said, "There is no house that they are recited in it, that does not find its protection with Allah s.w.t." Therefore, individuals who find themselves in need, will find that their needs are sufficed by these two verses. Umar r.a. knowing how much the Prophet s.a.w emphasised the blessings from these verses, said, "I am astonished that a person knows these two verses and does not recite them in their mornings and their evenings as a protection and healing from every ailment." We ask Allah s.w.t. to give us the wisdom and the practice of the *ṣaḥābah* and the Prophet Muhammad s.a.w.

Allah s.w.t. says,

$$ ءَامَنَ ٱلرَّسُولُ بِمَآ أُنزِلَ إِلَيْهِ مِن رَّبِّهِ وَٱلْمُؤْمِنُونَ $$

Allah s.w.t. begins these verses by showing love to the Prophet s.a.w., that the Messenger has demonstrated faith. It is as if Allah is counselling the *ṣaḥābah* that, "You should immediately believe what I have revealed to you, what I have said to you, that I am going to hold you accountable to what is in your heart, what is in your practice, that you should be willing to submit in it." The whole theme of Surah al-Baqarah is that there were those who would receive the verses and they would reject them. They would not practise them wholeheartedly and doubted Allah's orders. This was a theme that was the undoing of previous generations of those who were given the scripture from our Lord, s.w.t.

$$كُلٌّ ءَامَنَ بِالله$$

Allah said, the Prophet has demonstrated faith, now the believers must do so. Show our faith in Allah, the angels, the books and the Messengers.

$$لَا نُفَرِّقُ بَيْنَ أَحَدٍ مِّن رُّسُلِهِ$$

That Allah does not make separation between one Messenger and the next. Their messages have always been the same.

$$وَقَالُوا سَمِعْنَا وَأَطَعْنَا$$

All of them would say to us: "O' believer, I hear Allah and I obey. The negligence I have in my life, I'm going to change them. The things that I want to improve in, I will make efforts in them. The things that I know Allah has ordered, Allah has maintained and Allah has asked, I will do and fulfill them as best as I can. The constitution of a believer, I hear and I obey."

$$غُفْرَانَكَ رَبَّنَا وَإِلَيْكَ ٱلْمَصِيرُ (٢٨٥)$$

"My Lord, I remain asking you for forgiveness because

although I hear and obey, there will be negligence on my part, internally and externally. Therefore, I acknowledge that to You, I will return."

لَا يُكَلِّفُ ٱللهُ نَفْسًا إِلَّا وُسْعَهَا

Allah then gives us *husnu zhon*, to have good and high aspiration in Him. Allah says, "Don't you know that your Lord, Allah will never burden you? With that which you are unable to bear." Your first thought should have been, 'Our Lord would never burden us more than what we had.' This means that Allah is not going to judge us more than what we should be judged.

لَهَا مَا كَسَبَتْ وَعَلَيْهَا مَا ٱكْتَسَبَتْ

Allah has decided that whatever gain we have of good; it will be done. Then, whatever suffering that is of bad, it will be held accountable for. When we are confronted with an instruction from Allah, with an order that we are unable to perform, or something that we are scared of, we should immediately say:-

رَبَّنَا لَا تُؤَاخِذْنَا إِن نَّسِينَا أَوْ أَخْطَأْنَا ۚ رَبَّنَا وَلَا تَحْمِلْ عَلَيْنَا إِصْرًا كَمَا حَمَلْتَهُ عَلَى ٱلَّذِينَ مِن قَبْلِنَا ۚ رَبَّنَا وَلَا تُحَمِّلْنَا مَا لَا طَاقَةَ لَنَا بِهِ ۖ وَٱعْفُ

عَنَّا وَٱغْفِرْ لَنَا وَٱرْحَمْنَاۤ أَنتَ مَوْلَىٰنَا فَٱنصُرْنَا
عَلَى ٱلْقَوْمِ ٱلْكَـٰفِرِينَ (٢٨٦)

… so that we recognise that our Lord is never going to test us more than we can withstand.

رَبَّنَا لَا تُؤَاخِذْنَاۤ إِن نَّسِينَاۤ أَوْ أَخْطَأْنَاۚ

Remember, it begins with us knowing that Allah will never test us, or hold us accountable for that which we have forgotten, or that in which we have unintentionally made mistakes, and we have asked for His forgiveness. Make this *duʿāʾ*, "Do not hold us accountable for what we have forgotten, or what we have made a mistake in."

رَبَّنَا وَلَا تَحْمِلْ عَلَيْنَاۤ إِصْرًا كَمَا حَمَلْتَهُۥ عَلَى
ٱلَّذِينَ مِن قَبْلِنَاۚ

Our Lord, do not burden us with something that is beyond what we are able to withstand as You have burden like those who came before us.

رَبَّنَا وَلَا تُحَمِّلْنَا مَا لَا طَاقَةَ لَنَا بِهِۦۖ

Our Lord, do not test us more than what we are able to withstand, a burden that is greater for us to maintain in our life. We will find that the actions of worship and remembrance of God are all the things that are within our means to perform. For those acts that are obligatory upon us like our five daily prayers, fasting in the blessed month of Ramadan, *Alhamdulillah* they are within our means to fulfil. May Allah accept all of our actions.

وَٱعۡفُ عَنَّا

Our Lord, pardon us. It is not just asking Allah to forgive us, but to also pardon us, as if it never happened. We ask Allah to forgive us and show us mercy. *'Afuw* is pardon, as if it never happened.

وَٱغۡفِرۡ لَنَا

Ighfir means O' Allah, give me time to do good deeds that will cover up my sinful deeds.

وَٱرۡحَمۡنَآ

Warham, means show us mercy in the matters of which we are undeserving of Your Forgiveness.

أَنتَ مَوۡلَىٰنَا

You are our Lord, our master, our Allah.

فَٱنصُرۡنَا عَلَى ٱلۡقَوۡمِ ٱلۡكَٰفِرِينَ (٢٨٦)

Give us victory and ascendency. Give us aid against those who seek to wage war against You, Our Lord.

It is a powerful verse, but how do we apply it? In our mornings, in our evenings, at any time of weakness, at any time of illness, we can cup our hands, recite it and place it on our neck, our back, our knees, wherever we find that pain, make it a healing for our heart, reflect and ponder its meaning and go on a little bit deeper than these explanations. Make sure that the last two verses *Khawatim al-Baqarah* are done in tandem with *Āyatul Kursi* and that it is something that we recite and make as a daily routine.

We can also use it as a *ruqyah* for ourselves and our children. We can also make *du'ā'* in it, breathe on our hands and wipe it over our children. This is also from the practice of the successors of the Prophet s.a.w. and *'ulamā'* of the past and present. We ask Allah s.w.t. to give us the Treasure of Jannah that we practise in this life. Use it as a healing in our life. Make it our Ramadan therapy and that Allah s.w.t. accepts our fast and join us in Jannatul Firdaus with our Prophet Muhammad s.a.w. O' Allah, give us healing in all of our conditions in this blessed month of Ramadan, ya rabba al-amin.

Chapter 3

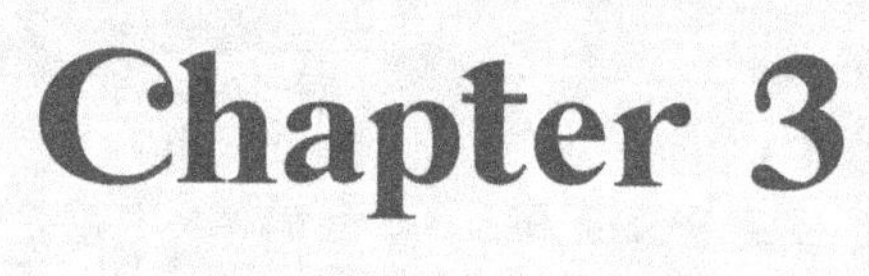

Salawat
upon Prophet
Muhammad
s.a.w.

اللَّهُمَّ صَلِّ عَلَى مُحَمَّدٍ وَعَلَى آلِ مُحَمَّدٍ

Allahumma ṣalli ʿala Muhammad wa ʿala āli Muhammad

O Allah, send ṣolah (blessing) upon Muhammad and upon the family of Muhammad (An-Nasa'i 1292)

One of the things Allah s.w.t. has equipped us with is the power of *duʿāʾ*. The ability to invoke Him s.w.t. and seek His blessings. Many times of course, we do not know what to ask for and we are asking for things that are not good for us. Therefore, one of the great secrets in our way of asking for what is truly best for us is to consider the needs of others. Our love for others is a pretext for earning the love of Allah, and then Allah will grant us what we seek of Him s.w.t.

There is none who deserves a greater love from those who walked the Earth than our Prophet Muhammad s.a.w. Allah s.w.t. says, "Surely it is God, Allah The Almighty who begins by sending His Mercy upon the Prophet s.a.w., His *Rahmah*."

It is invoked as a right of the Prophet s.a.w. that the angels in their totalities send their benedictions and greetings, asking Allah s.w.t. to send His Mercy upon our Prophet Muhammad s.a.w.

"O' ye who has come to faith, may Allah s.w.t. accept our prayers for him s.a.w. as a mercy upon him and reflect it back into our life and into goodness."

This is a very important concept that when we ask Allah s.w.t. selflessly for another individual, another human being, that Allah blesses their life, changes their condition, makes them from those who are fortunate—then in fact, Allah sends an angel who also answers that *du'ā'* by saying, *"Āmīn*, and to you as well" for what we have asked for our brother or our sister. Now consider that if we are making that *du'ā'* for someone who is more blessed than us, then what we have asked for them cascades into greater meaning and have greater effect in our life. No one is nearer to Allah s.w.t. than our Prophet s.a.w. Therefore, we want to send our benedictions, our *salawat* and our *durood* upon our Prophet Muhammad s.a.w.

"O' Allah, we send our blessings upon our Prophet s.a.w., asking You to send Your mercy and peace upon him from the first to the last and to mention him in the highest levels with You, O' Allah s.w.t."

When we fulfill this *solah* upon the Prophet s.a.w by saying:

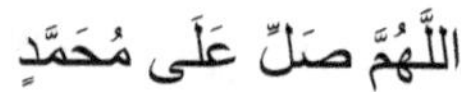

اللَّهُمَّ صَلِّ عَلَى مُحَمَّدٍ

We are not just doing something extra but—we are actually doing the bare minimum. The Prophet s.a.w. in an authentic *hadith* which he linked in explanation to the significance of the month of Ramadan, said that He heard Jibril make three *du'ā'*, two of which are relevant here. The first *du'ā* Jibril made was:

"O' Allah, the one who enters the month of Ramadan and does not earn your forgiveness, they have been cut off from the mercy of God." The Prophet s.a.w. responded with "*Āmīn*", sanctifying that *du'ā'*. Jibril then made the second *du'ā'*, "O' Messenger of Allah, the one who hears your name and doesn't send his blessings, benedictions, and prayers of peace for you, may they be cut off from the mercy of Allah." The Prophet s.a.w. again said "*Āmīn*". (Sahih Ibn Hibbān 915)

May Allah protect us from this. Therefore, the month of Ramadan and the *salawat* upon the Prophet s.a.w. are linked together through the words of our Prophet s.a.w in this hadith.

There was a man by the name of Ubay ibn Kaab r.a., who was among the great elite of the *ṣaḥābah*. He was one of the greatest reciters of the Qur'an and is in our chain of narration in the *mushaf*, as well as in our oral transmission. If we are to open the Qur'an and look at the very final pages, we will find that his name will be mentioned there, that this

Qur'an is with the *Riwāyat*, and they are—Ubay ibn Kaab, Uthman ibn Affan, Ali ibn Abi Talib and Zayd ibn Thabit. Consider therefore, the significance of who this man was.

He came to the Messenger of Allah s.a.w. asking,

"I often supplicate. When I supplicate, I devote some of my supplication to you, asking Allah to bless you, O' Messenger of Allah. Is this something praiseworthy?"

The Prophet s.a.w. said,

"Yes, and if you were to increase it, it's good."

"I'm going to do a quarter of my supplication for you, O' Messenger of Allah."

"This is blessed, but if you increase it, it's good."

"Half, O' Messenger of Allah."

"It's good, but if you increase it, it's better."

"Two thirds, out of every three *duʿā'*, two of them for you, O' Messenger of Allah."

"If you increase it, it's even better."

"O' Messenger of Allah, I will no longer ask about something for myself. Although I have a need, I'm not going to ask for or say what I want, I know Allah knows my heart and what I need, but I'm going to make my *ṣolah* out of love and devotion for you, O' Messenger of Allah, that I ask to send His peace and blessings be upon you. I will dedicate all of my supplication, its entirety, towards you O' Messenger of Allah."

Prophet s.a.w. then said,

"Then whatever it is that has been troubling you, will be sufficed. And whatever need that you have, will be fulfilled. And your sins will be forgiven." (At-Tirmidhi 2457)

This is narrated by Imam Ahmad and many others. It is an authentic *hadith* of the Prophet s.a.w.

There are thirty-nine blessings of sending benediction upon the Prophet s.a.w. This is only a summary of them, but for the first of them, we are responding to what has been ordered by Allah. Allah sends His blessings and His peace upon the Prophet s.a.w. as the angels asked for it. Allah tells us, O' ye, be like the angels and ask that for the Messenger of Allah s.a.w.

Therefore, we are following and responding to the order of Allah, and acting in the conduct of what the angels acted upon. Through that, we are attaining ten blessings. The Prophet s.a.w. said,

"The one who sends benediction upon me once, they will receive ten in reward." The Prophet s.a.w also said, "The one who sends blessings upon me, they will be elevated by ten levels in this *duniya* and in Jannah." Ten sins will be forgiven, and ten good deeds will be written in the record. (Sunan an-Nasa'i 1297)

Consequently, the thing that raises our *du'a'* to Allah is to raise *du'a'* for the one whose *du'a'* is always answered—Muhammad s.a.w. It is also a means to receive the intercession, the *shafaat* of the Prophet s.a.w. on the Day of Judgement. This is something that we seek on that fateful day. We ask Allah s.w.t. to grant us the *shafaat* of the Prophet s.a.w. when others seek it. It is also a means of one's sins being forgiven as we heard in the *hadith* of Ubay ibn Kaab r.a. It is a means of having our worldly needs that we know of and that we do not yet know of, fulfilled by Allah s.w.t. on account of us seeking to fulfill our love for Prophet Muhammad s.a.w.

It is also something that fulfils our internal and external needs and the needs of those we love and who are in love with us. It is a means of receiving the Prophet s.a.w's blessings as well as that of the angels, when they return our *salam*. Whenever we give *salam*, it is returned. The Prophet s.a.w. said in an authentic *hadith*,

"When a person makes *salam* upon me, Allah returns my soul to me, and I return the greeting back to you." (Sunan Abi Dawud 2041)

May Allah s.w.t. by means of our *salawat* upon Prophet Muhammad s.a.w, comfort us with the prayers and *shafaat* of the Prophet s.a.w. on the Day of Judgement. Some of the added blessings of the *salawat* is that it is an extermination of poverty. It allows us to fulfill the needs that we have in our worldly pursuits, food, and hunger. It is something that gives us strength in our body, and it will give us light on the *siratal mustaqim*. There are so many blessings in the *salawat* upon the Prophet s.a.w.—therefore, we should always include it in our daily *du'a'*.

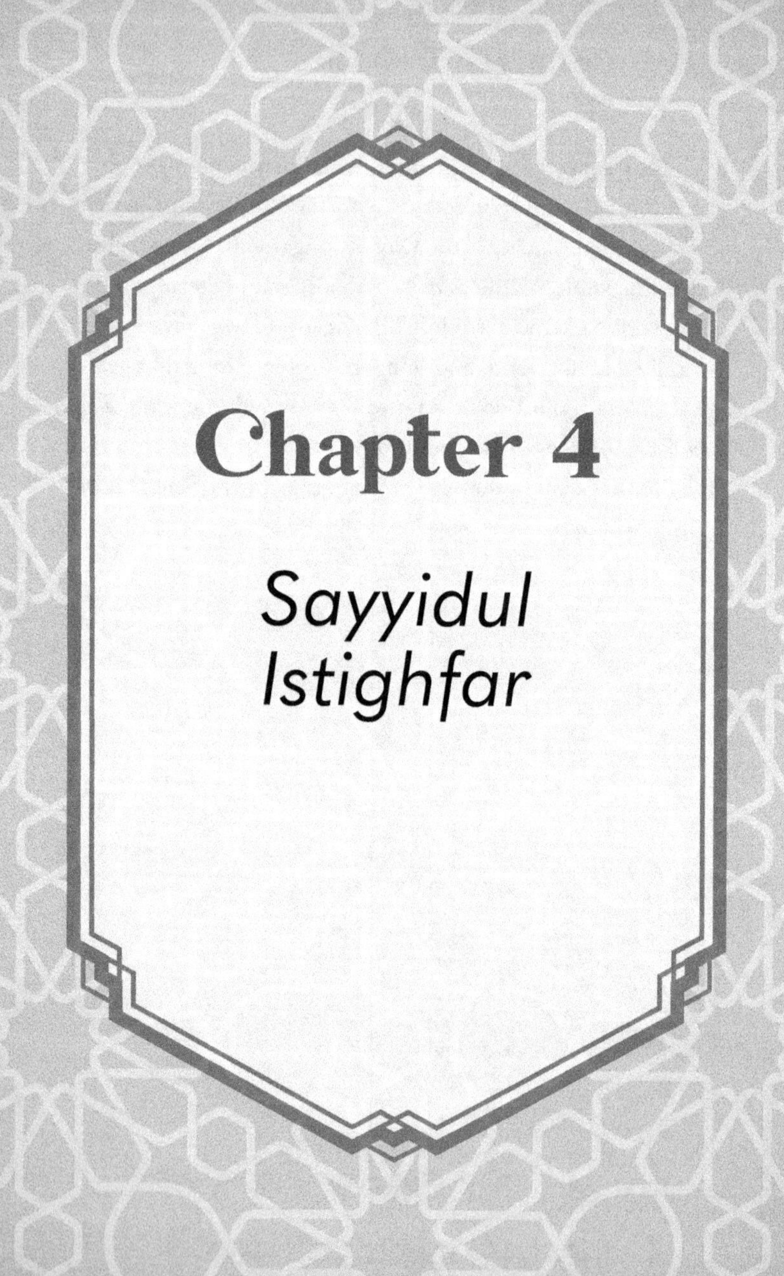

Chapter 4

Sayyidul Istighfar

اللَّهُمَّ أَنْـتَ رَبِّي، لاَ إِلَهَ إِلاَّ أَنْـتَ، خَلَقْتَـنِي وَأَنَا عَبْدُكَ، وَأَنَا عَلَى عَهْدِكَ وَوَعْدِكَ مَا اسْتَطَعْتُ، أَعُوذُ بِكَ مِنْ شَرِّ مَا صَنَعْتُ، أَبُوءُ لَكَ بِنِعْمَتِكَ عَلَيَّ وَأَبُـوءُ لَكَ بِذَنْـبِي، فَاغْفِـرْ لِي، فَإِنَّهُ لاَ يَغْفِرُ الذُّنُـوبَ إِلاَّ أَنْـتَ

Allahumma anta Rabbī lā ilaha illā anta, khalaqtanī wa anā ʿabduka, wa anā ʿala ʿahdika wa waʾadika mastaṭaʾatu, aʿūdhu bika min sharri mā ṣanaʾatu, abū uʾ laka binʾimatika ʿalaiyya, wa abū uʾ laka bidhanbi faghfir lī fa innahu lā yaghfiru adhdhunūba illā anta.

O Allah! You are my Lord. There is no true god except You. You have created me, and I am Your slave, and I hold to Your Covenant as far as I can. I seek refuge in You from the evil of what I have done. I acknowledge the favours that You have bestowed upon me, and I confess my sins. Pardon me, for none but You has the power to pardon. (Sahih Bukhari 6306)

The *du'ā'* that we are focusing on has a special title. The title is given by the greatest of *al-Anbiya*, Muhammad s.a.w. This is a *hadith* that is found in Sahih Bukhari in the chapter of *da'awat*, of the invocations of the Prophet Muhammad s.a.w. It comes from the *Riwāyat* of one of the great *ṣaḥabah*, Shaddad ibn Aus r.a., where he said,

"The chief, the head, the greatest way and the most superior way is asking for *istighfar*, for forgiveness..." (Sahih Bukhari 6306)

Now let us clarify the word *istighfar*. *Istighfar* is to ask Allah s.w.t. for forgiveness, it does not necessarily mean we are asking Allah to free us from our sins entirely, or that it is removed from our record. Rather, *istighfar* is for the things that we are unaware of. It is not the same as *tawbah*, although it is used similarly.

Tawbah means we know what we did wrong, we know what the sin is, so we are asking Allah for that particular sin to be forgiven. *Istighfar* is for the sins we have missed, have not paid attention to, and we are not aware of their gravity while they sneak up on us. As the Prophet s.a.w. said in a *hadith* concerning sins that are hidden—they are very silent and deadly, but they have a great effect, especially because they come in small amounts, but they can accumulate and become a massive error between us and Allah. (Jami' at-Tirmidhi 3530)

May Allah protect us.

However, *istighfar* is to cover up the sins that we have made, that we ask Allah to cover them up with the good deeds. We are asking Allah to give us a long enough life, to give us good enough *tawfiq* and providence, that we do enough good deeds that we will overwhelm these sinful deeds that we have made unknowingly and unintentionally, in occurrence between us and Allah and involving others. May Allah protect us from this.

Allah s.w.t. says,

"Righteous deeds, they extinguish, wipe away, cover over sinful deeds." (Jami' at-Tirmidhi 1987)

May Allah make us of those who wipe away our sinful deeds.

What is the *du'a'* we say? It begins by an admission when we say,

$$اللَّهُمَّ أَنْتَ رَبِّي،$$

O' Allah, You are my Lord. The Only One that I will worship.

$$لاَ إِلَهَ إِلاَّ أَنْتَ،$$

I have no one other than You, O' Allah.

خَلَقْتَنِي وَأَنَا عَبْدُكَ،

You are the One who created me, and I acknowledge You as my Creator, my Lord, my Sustainer, the Only One for me to worship. And I am Your slave.

وَأَنَا عَلَى عَهْدِكَ وَوَعْدِكَ مَا اسْتَطَعْتُ،

And I commit myself day and night that I will give You this commitment, this covenant as much as I am able to fulfill it.

Notice this *du'ā'* of the Prophet s.a.w., that our commitment to Allah s.w.t. is conditional to our ability. There will be times when we falter, but as long as we are able O' Allah, we will give this promise, this covenant to You.

أَعُوذُ بِكَ مِنْ شَرِّ مَا صَنَعْتُ،

I seek protection in You, Allah. I recognise that You are the Lord who is the Only One who can protect. And I recognise that these evil deeds are created within me and within others. That You, O' Allah s.w.t. have given me the capacity to make these mistakes and I will refer the same evilness of myself to me, not to You, O' Allah. I seek protection with You, in You and through You from that which I brought forth. From that which my hands have earned. From that which my tongue, eyes, ears, and limbs have brought myself to difficulties.

أَبُوءُ لَكَ بِنِعْمَتِكَ عَلَىَّ وَأَبُوءُ لَكَ بِذَنْبِي،

I turn to you, O' Allah, in an acknowledgment of the blessings, ni'mah You have given me.

Ni'mah is something that is given to us by Allah that we have not earned or worked towards. It is a grace from Allah that was not something we earned, we cannot stand and say, "I deserve it." For that Allah has blessed us even though we are unworthy of it. We acknowledge before You, we put before You, O' Allah, our sinfulness, our *dhanb*. The word *dhanb* is different from *khati-ah*. *Dhanb* is a mistake we knowingly made. *Khati-ah* is a mistake we made of which we do not know its gravity or its error.

I ask you Allah and I put forward to you from the sins that I know, and I do not know.....

فَاغْفِرْ لِي،

Forgive it for me, O' Allah. Give me the time, the energy, the ability to cover it over with good deeds. Give me the life that I can make up this error that I have made, this sinfulness that I have.

فَإِنَّهُ لاَ يَغْفِرُ الذُّنُوبَ إِلاَّ أَنْتَ

For no one is able to forgive the sins, except You, O' Allah. No one is able to allow me this opportunity to gain days and moments of my life, to be able to expel it from my record. To work righteous deeds and to have the ability to please You, O' Allah so that I can cover over these sins.

There is only You, O' Allah. No one is capable of forgiving except You, O' Allah.

The Prophet s.a.w. said,

"The one who says this in his day and is to pass away before the night, before going to sleep, they are given Jannah. The one says at its night and passes away before he wakes up, then they are from the people of Jannah." (Sahih Bukhari 6306)

They will be given the reward of Jannah by the testimony of the Prophet s.a.w. They will be from its people, *SubhanAllah*. Make that *du'ā'* when we wake up and as a part of the days that we have in the month of Ramadan.

Why is this *du'ā'* really important? First, see the construction. We acknowledge the greatness of Allah. We acknowledge our weakness before Him. We acknowledge that no one is capable of forgiving, but Him. We acknowledge that all supremacy, all might is within His Hand. We acknowledge that He is the Only One that we turn to in need and in sorrow or pain, happiness or joy, and all our conditions.

O' Allah, You are the source of everything that is good and we are the ones who have brought corruption into our life, and if we return to a place of righteousness with You, O' Allah, we are confident that the said corruption we brought will no longer remain. We understand You are our Creator, our Maker, our Fashioner, You are the One who brought us into this world. You are the One who destined this life and this existence. You are the One who has given us these trials, tests and tribulations. You are the Only One therefore, that we will worship.

We understand that to be the slave of Allah is nobility, to be a slave of anything else is a humiliation. However, when we give our enslavement willingly to Allah s.w.t., the power that would be stripped of us is given to us in many folds through the strength provided to us by Allah.

A slave is therefore the one whose powers are usurped, when they give their enslavement to other than God. Yet, when we are a slave of Allah, Allah's power extends toward us in that He becomes the sight that we see with, the hearing we hear with and the strength that we possess in our hand.

Therefore, Allah says to us in this authentic *hadith* narrated by Bukhari and Muslim, where the Prophet s.a.w. reports that Allah s.w.t said,

Ramadan Therapy

"When I love him I am his hearing with which he hears, his seeing with which he sees, his hand with which he strikes and his foot with which he walks." (Hadith Qudsi 25)

This means that what will please Allah for us to see, we will see. What is displeasing, we will turn away from because of our consciousness in Him. We ask Allah s.w.t. to make *sayyidul istighfar*, this greatest way for us to seek forgiveness from Allah s.w.t., as a part of our morning and evening routine in the month of Ramadan and to even extend beyond the month of Ramadan.

Chapter 5

Gaining Strength and Resilience

Ramadan Therapy

اَللهُ أَكْبَرْ

Allahu Akbar x33

Allah is the Greatest

سُبْحَانَ اللَّه

SubḥānAllah x34 or x33

Glorified be Allah

اَلْحَمْدُلِلَّه

Alḥamdulillah x33

All praises are for Allah

(Sahih Bukhari 3113)

This *du'ā'* is from a *hadith* that is in Sahih Bukhari, in the book of *da'awat*. It is a beautiful *hadith* narrated by Ali ibn Abi Talib r.a., who was speaking as the husband of the daughter of the Prophet Muhammad s.a.w., Fatimah az-Zahraa r.a. Ali r.a narrated that Fatimah was complaining about the difficulty of raising two children, Hasan and Husain who were born soon after each other. She was not feeling well, she had a physical pain and was lacking in strength.

Fatimah came to the house of the Prophet s.a.w to ask for someone to assist her, as a servant. Someone that the Prophet could intercede on her behalf and say, "Look, can you help my daughter out a little bit?" She did not find the Prophet s.a.w at home, so she mentioned her pain and difficulties to 'Ā'ishah r.a., who promised to inform the Prophet s.a.w when he returned home. Immediately upon the Prophet s.a.w. returning home, 'Ā'ishah r.a informed him of Fatimah's complaint and the Prophet immediately went to them, although they (Ali and Fatimah) had already entered their room.

Ali r.a. said, "We were already laying down to sleep when the Prophet s.a.w came. Fatimah opened the door and I stood up to get out of bed and greet him and the Prophet s.a.w. said, 'Stay where you are.'" "The Prophet sat between us" said Ali r.a. Fatimah and Ali were facing the Prophet s.a.w when he then sat in front of them. Ali said, "I could feel the radiance and coolness of the Prophet s.a.w.'s face, even into my chest." Prophet s.a.w. was sitting near them facing them and the strength, the beauty, and the coolness of the Prophet s.a.w. radiated from him that Ali r.a could feel the coolness in his chest.

The Prophet s.a.w. began immediately, "Do you want me to tell the both of you that which will be of greater benefit to you than if I were to assign someone to assist you in your home?" The Prophet then said, **"If both of you come to your bed..."**

Now this is something that is important for us and our spouse, as we both get into bed together. We should try to avoid the practice of one of us going to bed and the other staying up late at night for whatever reason. Come into the room together, share the bed together, enjoy each other's company together and retire together.

The Prophet s.a.w. then said, "When you both come to bed to each other, and you've laid down gotten into bed, you're rested and you're not getting up for anything else, then say your takbir, say *Allahu Akbar*, thirty-three times. Then say *SubhanAllah* thirty-three times. Then say *Alhamdulillah* thirty-three times. This will be more beneficial for you than if I were to give you and assign for you a servant." (Sahih Bukhari 3113)

In another narration, it is said that we should say our tasbih, *SubhanAllah* thirty-four times, meaning to end it at thirty-four times rather than thirty-three. Therefore, say *SubhanAllah* thirty-four times, then *Allahu Akbar* thirty-three times, followed by *Alhamdulillah* thirty-three times. This was mentioned to his cousin, Ali ibn Abi Talib and Fatimah, the daughter of Prophet Muhammad s.a.w. This is sure proof for a method of gaining strength, finding resilience, and finding an ability to continue throughout our days and nights. The Prophet s.a.w. said, "If you say this in the evening, you will not need anyone to assist you or to provide help for you."

May Allah grant us strength, and we ask Allah to make us of those who practise this great *sunnah*.

Chapter 6
Attaining Allah's
Forgiveness

قُـلْ: اللَّهُمَّ إِنِّي ظَلَمْـتُ نَفْـسِي ظُلْمًا كَثِيرًا، وَلاَ

يَغْفِـرُ الذُّنُـوبَ إِلَّا أَنْـتَ، فَاغْفِـرْ لِي مَغْفِـرَةً مِنْ

عِنْـدِكَ، وَارْحَمْـنِي إِنَّكَ أَنْـتَ الغَفُـورُ الرَّحِيمُ

Qul: Allahumma inni zolamtu nafsi zulman kathiran, wa lā yaghfirudh-dhunūba illā Anta, faghfir lī maghfiratan min 'indika, warhamnī, innaka Antal-Ghafūrur-Rahim

Say: O' Allah! I have considerably wronged myself. There is none to forgive the sins but You. So grant me pardon and have mercy on me. You are The Most Forgiving, The Most Compassionate. (Riyad as-Salihin 1475)

This *du'ā'* is a very powerful *du'ā'*. This *du'ā'* is a form of invocation and supplication that was prescribed to one of the dearest companions of Prophet Muhammad s.a.w. This *hadith* is narrated by Abdullah ibn Amr al-'Aas, who was one of the elite *sahib*, but he said, I heard, Abu Bakr as-Siddiq r.a., asking the Prophet s.a.w.; this *hadith* is in Sahih Bukhari in the book of invocations.

Abdullah ibn Amr al-'Aas said, I heard Abu Bakr r.a.

saying, "O' Messenger of God, teach me an invocation that I can call upon Allah s.w.t. with it, during my prayers." It is as if Abu Bakr r.a. is saying, "O' Messenger of Allah, I know how to say other *dhikrs*, but I want something special, something unique. I want something that you will give to me that is going to elevate my *solah*, that is going to make it better. I don't want something long, because I'm not reading a long thing, I want something that is going to hone to my specific needs." Then Prophet s.a.w. said to him, "Qul", say:

قُلْ: اللَّهُمَّ إِنِّي ظَلَمْتُ نَفْسِي ظُلْمًا كَثِيرًا،

It begins with us making an admission. "O' my Lord, I have wronged myself in many ways." *SubhanAllah*, this harkens to the *du'ā'* of Adam a.s. when he ate from the forbidden tree. Adam a.s and Hawaa a.s. said,

"Our Lord, we have wronged ourselves, and if You do not forgive us and have mercy upon us, we will surely be among the losers." (Surah al-A'raf: Verse 23)

It is in the constitution of a believer, that when we come to Allah, we come with an admission of our inequities, our sins, and our faults, because we do not seek repentance from anyone other than Allah. We do not have this tradition where we will speak to someone on behalf of us to Allah. We speak directly to Allah. It is as if we are conversing with

Allah. The Prophet s.a.w. said, *Qul*—say (the *du'ā'* above) O'
Abu Bakr.

Acknowledge our mistakes, our sins and our errors.
SubhanAllah Abu Bakr r.a. was a pious man, he was a man
of righteousness. He was good enough to accompany the
Prophet s.a.w. when others were not able to. He accompanied
the Prophet in the cave, in the journey of migration. He was
the first to come to faith. He was the foundation of so much
good in our *deen* and he became the first *khalifah* after the
Prophet s.a.w. returned to Allah.

Nevertheless, the Prophet s.aw. said, "Acknowledge your
mistakes." The mistakes of Abu Bakr to us in our eyes are the
size of pebbles, but to him, they were the size of mountains.

$$ \text{وَلاَ يَغْفِرُ الذُّنُوبَ إِلَّا أَنْتَ،} $$

After admitting our fault, elevate and magnify Allah.
"My Lord, no one will forgive, no one can forgive, no one
is capable of forgiving so much, other than You, O' Allah.
The multiplicity of my errors, except You, O' Allah." This
is another way of saying, "There is not one to turn to except
You, O' Allah." There is no one we ask for help except You,
O' Allah. There is no one that we can turn to in our pain,
sufferings, mistakes, and sins, except You, O' Allah. No one
can make forgiveness of these sins for us, except You.

فَاغْفِرْ لِي مَغْفِرَةً مِنْ عِنْدِكَ،

"Therefore, my Lord, forgive me. A forgiveness that is only from You. Forgive me, a forgiveness only from You. Only You, O 'Allah."

Whenever we use Only You, we know that it is a special thing. Allah s.w.t. says that whenever we refer it back to Allah s.w.t., we are asking for something greater than what others can assume. Only from You, O' Allah. Something that is specific that is not given to anybody else.

وَارْحَمْنِي إِنَّكَ أَنْتَ الْغَفُورُ الرَّحِيمُ

"O' my Lord show me *rahmah*." Therefore, there is a difference between *maghfirah* and *rahmah*. *Maghfirah* is where we ask of Allah s.w.t. to forgive us for our inequity. *Rahmah* is where we seek Allah's Mercy that He does not just forgive us and give us time to make up for those sins but He forgives us and then shows us His Mercy as if we have not committed those sins. We ask Allah s.w.t. for His *maghfirah*. We ask Allah for His *rahmah*. "O' Allah, forgive me from Your forgiveness, something only from You and show me Your *rahmah*, Your Mercy, Compassion, Your Love, O' Allah."

إِنَّكَ أَنْتَ الْغَفُورُ الرَّحِيمُ

Then join the two words, *Ghafur* and *Rahim* together.

"Surely You Allah, are the Only One who shows forgiveness and is capable of that level of compassion and mercy." The Mercy of Allah s.w.t., Him being *ar-Rahman* and *ar-Rahim*, are the greatest qualities of Allah s.w.t. He introduced it to us in the beginning, *Bismillahirrahmanirrahim*, in the opening chapter of acquainting us with Him. *Ar-Rahman* is the only word that is mentioned in the name of Allah s.w.t. that is used on its own. It is sufficient in itself, therefore we seek the *Rahmah*, the compassion, the mercy, the graciousness and the forgiveness of Allah s.w.t. Learn, memorise, and repeat this invocation in our *solah*, especially in Ramadan to make it a Ramadan of therapy.

Chapter 7

Alleviating Harm
and Distress

لَا إِلَهَ إِلاَّ اللَّهُ الْحَلِـيمُ الْعَظِيمِ لَا إِلَهَ إِلاَّ اللَّهُ رَبُّ السَّمَوَاتِ وَرَبُّ الأَرْضِ لَا إِلَهَ إِلاَّ اللَّهُ رَبُّ الْعَرْشِ الْكَرِيمِ

Lā ilaha illallahul Ḥalīmul ʿAzīm, lā ilaha illallahu Rabbussamawāti wa Rabbul arḍi, lā ilaha illallahu Rabbul ʿArshil Karīm

There is none worthy of worship but Allah, the Forbearing, the Mighty. There is none worthy of worship but Allah, Lord of the Magnificent Throne. There is none worthy of worship but Allah, Lord of the Heavens and Lord of the Earth, and Lord of the Noble Throne. (Jami` at-Tirmidhi 3435)

***

This particular *duʿā'* is from the *hadith* of Abdullah ibn Abbas r.a. He was related to the Prophet s.a.w., and a young man for whom the Prophet s.a.w. in particular made lots of *duʿā'*. The Prophet s.a.w. said, "O' Allah, give Abdullah ibn Abbas an understanding of the Qur'an, its meanings and its dictates and its practice." Abdullah ibn Abbas lived for a long period of time where he was able to give victory to Islam and the *sunnah* of the Prophet s.a.w. He was a reference point in understanding the word of Allah, after the demise of the Prophet Muhammad s.a.w. and his return to Allah s.w.t. May Allah join us with him in the highest level of Jannah.

Because Abdullah ibn Abbas was related to the Prophet s.a.w., he used to be able to come into the household of the Prophet s.a.w. when other *ṣaḥābah* could not. He would sit with the Prophet s.a.w. in the evenings, at night, in the mornings, in the daytime. He was a person who was privy to the inner life of Prohet s.a.w. Since he was also young in age, he was able to observe things around the Prophet s.a.w for a number of years. He did not travel away from the Prophet s.a.w. He was not out working, buying, and selling. He was free during his young age to study and receive tutelage from the Prophet s.a.w. The Prophet s.a.w gave him this *duʿā'* and Abdullah ibn Abbas said the Prophet s.a.w. used to say it often whenever distress would arrive, so we should pay attention to it.

This becomes one of those central *duʿā'* that we need to know on how to alleviate harm, distress, feelings of foreboding, physical distress and financial distress. All those things that are considered *karb*. We ask Allah to undo the harm and distress we are facing. The Prophet s.a.w. would invariably say often in his life:

لاَ إِلَهَ إِلاَّ اللهُ الْعَظِيمِ الْحَلِيمُ

He would begin with the testimony of faith, the *shahādah* —the greatest, most beautiful word and the blessed word. It is the best statement that anyone has said, including the Prophets of the past, our Prophet and what was taught to us. It is the central focus of our *tawhid*, of our theology of faith of singling out only Allah s.w.t. and the more we repeat it, the better off we are. We will find that many of our foundational *hadith* and verses of the Qur'an are built from this statement. The greatest verse of the Qur'an, *Āyatul Kursi*, begins with this statement. It negates all aspects of worship of anything other than God and establishes only Allah s.w.t. Only to Allah will we turn to and worship, which is the basis of our faith, our Qur'an, and the basis of Surah al-Fātihah. Only You, Allah, do we worship, only You Allah, do we ask for help.

لاَ إِلَهَ إِلاَّ اللهُ

From that statement of the *shahādah*, four words, we will establish both. Nothing will we turn to, nothing will we seek support from, nothing will we ask for help or assistance, nothing will we believe has any power, benefit or harm or good for us, except Allah s.w.t. Why? This is because He is *al-Halīm, al-ʿAzīm*. He is The Almighty; *al-ʿAzīm*. Yet, He is also *al-Halīm*, The One who is patient in His dealings with us. The word *Halīm* comes from the word *hilm*, where Allah s.w.t. has a forbearance for us. He allows us to make our mistakes and return to Him. He gives us time to readjust. In all the circumstances in our life, He is gentle with us.

Therefore, the best of translations is that He is gentle in His forbearance and is patient over us. He is *al-'Azīm*, The Mighty, The Greatest, The One who is capable of doing and establishing what He orders, but He is *al-Halīm*. He is the one who gives us an opportunity to adjust ourselves. The word *Halīm* here implies that the Prophet s.a.w. is teaching us that we know there are indiscretions in our life which are the root cause of our distress.

The Prophet s.a.w. wants us to know that Allah is the Almighty and that He can extract and exact whatever He seeks of us, but He has *hilm*. Thus, if we truly believe that there is no God but Allah; if we understand this statement and we know His Might, then know that whatever patience Allah has given, having dealt with us through *as-Sabūr*, with His *Hilm*, do not take it for granted. He is *al-'Azīm, al-Halīm*. The Prophet s.a.w. repeats it, "No one is there for me to worship except Allah." Who is The Lord of all that is in the Heaven and the Earth. Therefore, whatever pain we have is part of this Heaven and this Earth. Whatever we believe that is too much for us or others to fix, Allah is able to fix. Whatever harm that we believe is too great, it can be undone with His s.w.t.'s power, mercy, and love.

لاَ إِلَـهَ إِلاَّ اللهُ رَبُّ السَّمَوَاتِ وَرَبُّ الأَرْضِ لاَ إِلَـهَ إِلاَّ اللهُ رَبُّ الْعَرْشِ الْكَرِيمِ

He is The Lord of the Heavens and the Earth. The Only Governor and Sustainer. The Innovator, The Creator. The One whose Existence brought about the existence of the Heavens and the Earth. He is the Lord of *al-'Arsh*, The Most Mighty, in its magnificence. *SubhanAllah*. In the *hadith* of the '*Arsh*', it is best not to translate it as a throne, as we do not want this kind of anthropomorphism. The *'Arsh* of *ar-Rahmān* is a creation from Allah s.w.t. that He has established for Himself.

In many places in the Qur'an, Allah s.w.t has stated that in His Majestic Presence, He rises above His *'Arsh*, in a way that is distinct from any of His creations. He is unique in Himself s.w.t. However, when the people would ask the Prophet s.a.w. about Allah s.w.t's *al-Kursi* in *Āyatul Kursi*, there are narrations where the Prophet s.a.w. said that all of the Heavens and the Earth, everything that exists including this universe and the multiverse, is like a ring in its size that is thrown into the vast open desert.

Imagine throwing a single ring into the Sahara Desert. All of the Heavens and creation are the size of this ring, compared to the magnificence of Allah s.w.t's *al-Kursi*. Now imagine the size of the *'Arsh* of *ar-Rahmān*. The Prophet s.a.w has said that the *Kursi* is like a ring compared to the *'Arsh*. (Sahih Ibn Hibban; al-Ihsan 361)

The *'Arsh* is so magnificent in its presence and establishment. Above the *'Arsh*, in a manner that befits His Majesty, having might, power, and authority over all of His creations, is Allah s.w.t. He is the Lord of *al-'Arsh* which is *'Azīm*, which is beyond the description of magnificence. This is a *du'ā'* that would be recited by the Prophet s.a.w. at times of difficulty. It reminds him of the greatness, power, and authority of Allah. It is to remind us of the presence of Allah in our lives, and to remind us as to who we turn to for help and assistance—from whom we seek blessings and assistance.

Chapter 8

Diminishing Harms of the Past, Present and Future

اللَّهُـمَّ إِنِّي أَعُوذُ بِـكَ مِـنَ الْبُخْـلِ، وَأَعُوذُ بِـكَ مِـنَ الْجُبْنِ، وَأَعُوذُ بِـكَ أَنْ أُرَدَّ إِلَى أَرْذَلِ الْعُمُـرِ، وَأَعُوذُ بِـكَ مِـنْ فِثْنَةِ الدُّنْيَا يَعْنِي فِثْنَةَ الدَّجَّالِ وَأَعُوذُ بِـكَ مِـنْ عَذَابِ الْقَـبْرِ

Allahumma innī a'udhu bika minal bukhli, wa a'udhu bika minal jubni, wa a'udhu bika an uradda ilay ardhalil 'umuri, wa a'udhu bika min fitnatid dunyā ya'anī finatid dajjāli, wa a'udhu bika min 'adhābil qabri

O' Allah! I seek refuge with You from miserliness; and seek refuge with You from cowardice; and seek refuge with You from being sent back to geriatric old age; and I seek refuge with You from the affliction of this world (i.e., the affliction of ad-Dajjal etc.); and seek refuge with You from the punishment of the grave." (Sahih al-Bukhari 6365)

This is a really precious *du'ā'* to those who are undergoing different constraints in life. This is from the *du'ā'* of *jami*, meaning a comprehensive *du'ā'*. One of the gifts given by Allah to the Prophet s.a.w. is that he was given the 'conciseness of speech and prayers' that covers vast meaning in such a comprehensive way with a few short words.

Saad r.a. narrated this *hadith* in Sahih Bukhari. Mus'ab r.a. reports from Saad, that Saad r.a. used to give reminders of five statements from the Prophet s.a.w., and that they were reminders he would see from Prophet s.a.w. They were five *du'ā'* that Saad would teach his disciples, his friends and family. (Sahih al-Bukhari 6365) He would say, "Don't take this from me, but this was from the Prophet Muhammad s.a.w." These were things that the Prophet Muhammad s.a.w. would pray for, regularly, consistently, day in day out, in accordance with the needs of his life. The Prophet s.a.w. would say,

اللَّهُمَّ إِنِّي أَعُوذُ بِكَ مِنَ الْبُخْلِ،

O' Allah, I ask you to protect me and I ask you to give me refuge and to turn to me away from al-Bukhl—from my miserliness.

To be *bakhil* is for someone who has but will not give; will not spend on themselves or on others. More particularly in this *du'ā'*, it is not just about not being a person who is unwilling to give, but to also not live with others who are unwilling to give. We do not want to be married to someone who does not spend, or would not spend, in that which is equitable, in that which is fair and asked for by Allah s.w.t. In addition, Allah s.w.t. said that from the traits of the humble servants of Allah who have firmness of faith in Him, they are those who when they come to spend, they do not spend excessively in an exaggerated sense, but at the same time they are not tightfisted (not willing to give or spend).

The worshippers of *ar-Rahmān* are those who are justly balanced. *Bakhīl* is someone who is beyond that balance, they are those who are tightfisted, unwilling to give. Therefore, the Prophet s.a.w. said, "Those who are miserly of people, are the ones who when my name is mentioned in front them and they do not send benedictions and blessings upon me." (Sahīh Ibn Hibbān 915) People who are not willing to spend in giving benedictions which is just and actable are miserly people or living amongst people who are miserly.

وَأَعُوذُ بِكَ مِنَ الْجُبْنِ،

"And I ask You to protect me from cowardice—from being a coward." Cowardice is the root cause of many pains we endure in life. Sometimes we are too weak, too cowardly to speak up for ourselves, to ask for our own rights. Sometimes we are too weak to ask for something that is attainable—if only we had asked, it would be given. Cowardice is fear that has gone beyond what is acceptable. Allah always cautioned the Prophet s.a.w. that fear is not something that is disliked in and of itself. Fear is a natural emotion, but if it controls us and keeps us from attaining that which we can, that is cowardice.

Therefore, Allah said to Musa a.s. and Harun a.s., *la tahaf*, don't you both be scared. To Dawud a.s., when he got scared. When Ibrahim a.s. saw the three angels, he was scared—*la tahaf*. Do not be fearful, do not let it make us cowards, that we cower away, we turn our back from that which is right. We stand up and speak a word of justice when it is necessary. This is so that we are able to give on a path that is just, to put ourselves on the line and to protect others that are both near and far. O' Allah, we ask You to save us from being miserly, from being a person of cowardice and a person whose fear controls every aspect of his life.

$$وَأَعُوذُ بِكَ أَنْ أُرَدَّ إِلَى أَرْذَلِ الْعُمُرِ،$$

"And I pray O' Allah, that You would not let me live to such a degree that I enter into a state of dementia of the mind, where I revert to not knowing who I am, where I belong, and who I worship."

To be in a state where we have lost consciousness, that we revert to being as if we were just born, as if we are a newborn in our adulthood, in our mental capacity. This is an insightful *du'ā'* of the Prophet s.a.w. In this *du'ā'*, we are not asking Allah to take our life or to end it, but for as long as the world has good for us, to let us live and do good, and to end our life in that state of goodness. But if our life is better that we return to You, O' Allah, then take us. Relieve us from it. We ask Allah s.w.t. not to give us the pain of geriatrics, where we are a burden to ourselves and upon others, that we leave this world with our mind and faculties intact.

وَأَعُوذُ بِكَ مِنْ فِتْنَةِ الدُّنْيَا يَعْنِي فِتْنَةَ الدَّجَّالِ

"And I ask you Allah to protect me from the *fitnah* of *duniya, fitnah* of *Dajjal*." To protect us from the lustful leaning that we will have in the *duniya*. From the desirous nature that we have from this worldly life. There is nothing wrong with being wealthy or to seek wealth or excess in that regard, as long as we earn it from the halal and spend it on the halal. To be *az-Zuhud* means to be a person who relinquishes love of the *duniya*, of this worldly life. It means that we own the world, we own possessions in it, but we do not let those things own us. We will not change our financial structures and what is ethical in our financial dealings to attain the *duniya*, by doing that which is haram, entering into *riba'*, sinful loans and so on. We will not change what is haram into halal to attain the *duniya*, just on account of that.

The Prophet s.a.w. said, "There has not been a Prophet before me from the time of Adam until now who has not warned his people of this false deity who will come and ask to be worshipped instead of God." The *Dajjal* is a man who will be coming out in our *ummah* and he will be followed by a vast majority of people, even from amongst those of us who claim to faith. Those who have hypocritical faith will follow him. Al-Madinah will shake and shudder as the Dajjal will not be able to enter it nor into Makkah Al-Mukarramah or Masjid Al-Aqsa, which will always be with the believers, may Allah continue to keep it blessed.

The *Dajjal* is a person who represents a devilish construct. He will be a person who will be given particular powers of illusion that will cause people during the times of drought and famine to follow him, because they believe he will give them prosperity, when in fact, it is actually adversity and sinfulness. May Allah protect us from the *Dajjal*.

وَأَعُوذُ بِكَ مِنْ عَذَابِ الْقَبْرِ

Lastly, the fifth *du'ā'*—"Protect me from the punishment of the grave." It is a reality, a part of our *aqidah*, that there is a punishment for the body and soul in the grave. It is in the belief of *Ahlil Sunnah* that the grave is a place that can become a garden from the gardens of paradise or a pit from the pits of the hellfire. We ask Allah s.w.t. to send light upon the ones that have departed and relieve them from the punishment. The Prophet s.a.w said there are 30 verses that are recited (and many recite Surah al-Mulk), where the one who recites them will be protected from the punishment of the grave. We should make it a part of our routines every night, along with the *du'ā'* above, as our daily practice to alleviate harm in the past, present and into the future.

Chapter 9

Protecting
Future
Offspring

Ramadan Therapy

$$\text{بِسْمِ اللَّهِ اللَّهُمَّ جَنِّبْنَا الشَّيْطَانَ وَجَنِّبِ الشَّيْطَانَ مَا رَزَقْتَنَا}$$

Bismillah, Allahumma jannibna-ash-shaiṭān, wa jannibi-ash-shaiṭāna mā razaqtanā

In the name of Allah, O' Allah protect us against Satan and keep away the Satan from the one that you have bestowed upon us. (Sahih Muslim 1434)

———◆———

The *hadith* and *duʿāʾ* are from Sahih Bukhari, the book of *da'awat*. We have been focusing on some of the authentic narrations of the Prophet s.a.w. and we are also going to study some verses of the Qur'an that are also pertinent in our invocations to Allah s.w.t. However, this one is particularly for those who *Alhamdulillah,* have entered into fulfilment of half of their deen—those who are married. May Allah s.w.t. bring happiness between a husband and wife. One of the ways to instill happiness is to have regular visitations and conjugal visits where we are together not just intimately, but also sexually. There is a difference between intimacy and sexuality.

'Ā'ishah r.a. said that among the things she missed the most after the departure of Prophet Muhammad s.a.w. was that he would bring his fingers into her fingers whenever he sat next to her and hold them together. 'Ā'ishah r.a. said that she would miss those intimate details of the Prophet s.a.w. that when she would raise a cup to drink, he would ask for the cup and she would see that he would look at her and make sure that she acknowledged that he drank from the same spot that her lips had drank from. These are levels of intimacy between a husband and wife that we need to increase in our blessed homes. May Allah s.w.t. fill our homes with *barakah, khayr,* happiness and merriment and disband the *shaytān* from around it.

Yet, one of the most strained aspects of marital life are the sexual encounters and coming together in love and comfort with each other. At times it can be strained if one is not protected from the *shaytān.* Therefore, the Prophet s.a.w. taught this *hadith* that was narrated by Abdullah ibn Abbas r.a. who was a young man and not yet married. It shows us that this topic is not taboo, and understand that as Muslims, sometimes we are very closed, and we feel that there is some inappropriateness when discussing such intimate matters openly. However, the Prophet s.a.w. was very progressive in outlook for his time that we find some of these *hadiths* were narrated by men and women, young men and women, even by those who were not yet married at the time.

Abdullah ibn Abbas r.a. narrated that the Prophet s.a.w. said, "If any one you, whenever they wish to have a conjugal visitation, comfort with their husband or with their wife." (Sahih Muslim 1434) In particular, if a man comes and he is about to enter upon his wife and they are about to enjoy each other's company intimately, he should say, "Bismillah". The word bismillah is always a foundation to remove the *shaytān* from our homes as we enter it, from our food as we partake from it, from our clothing as we put it on or take it off. All of these things were taught to us by the Prophet s.a.w. It is also a statement that turns the attention of the angels away from us during this particularly intimate act.

The Prophet s.a.w. said in an authentic *hadith*, that the angels turn away from us—even the ones who record our deeds, out of humility and shyness when we enter into the bathroom to fulfill our needs in that sense, when we enter upon our spouses and when we remove our clothing. However, the *shaytān* seeks to come during those private moments. Therefore, every time during each of these three instances, the Prophet s.a.w. taught us a *duʿā'*to blind the *shaytān*, to blind the nefarious, unseen forces from our presence. He said, as a way of protecting our home, spouse, ourselves, our future progeny and children, that we should say:

بِسْمِ اللهِ اللَّهُمَّ جَنِّبْنَا الشَّيْطَانَ

O' Allah, turn the *shaytān* away from us

وَجَنِّبِ الشَّيْطَانَ مَا رَزَقْتَنَا

And turn the *shaytān* away from that which may come as a *rizq* from this union

That if we are to be blessed with a child, turn the *shaytān* away from them, do not let the *shaytān* have a presence in their lives. The Prophet s.a.w. said, "If it is their *qadr* that they are to have a child out of meeting in this union, the devil will not have an evil presence, an evil lifestyle built upon them."

Now this is very important. The Prophet s.a.w. taught us to protect ourselves from the *shaytān*, to protect our spouse from the *shaytān*, to protect our unborn child if it was our *qadr*, if we were to have them in our life. This is a therapy we are all in need of. May Allah s.w.t. give us happiness, and it is something we should think about before we enter into that wonderful, blessed moment of enjoining each other in comfort and love, intimacy, and sexual activity. Once again, the Prophet would teach us to say, bismillah, which is always a *du'ā'* to say whenever we are going to do something good. Know that when a man enters upon his woman, when a woman and her husband find comfort in each other, that is an active charity, it is an act that earns a massive reward.

Ramadan Therapy

The *'ulamā'* say the reward of that act is equal to the amount of sinfulness if it was done outside of a marriage union. That shows us the gravity of the act compared to *zina* or adultery. It can be considered fornication on the one hand, and finding comfort and love with one's spouse on the other hand, which earns a massive amount of reward. How do we earn the maximum reward? Begin with this *du'ā'* of the Prophet s.a.w. O' Allah, we begin in everything that is blessed with Your name, seeking Your blessing. O' Allah, turn the *shaytān* away from us, blind him from us, keep him out of our presence, protect our children and our future children that may come from this union, from the influence of the *shaytān*. The Prophet s.a.w. said, if this was to happen, the *shaytān* will never be able to have presence upon nor to harm the child's life. May Allah s.w.t. protect our children, our homes and raise us up upon the *sunnah* of Prophet Muhammad s.a.w.

Chapter 10

Exchange for Those Who Have Been Wronged

اللَّهُمَّ فَأَيُّمَا مُؤْمِنٍ سَبَبْتُهُ فَاجْعَلْ ذَلِكَ لَهُ قُرْبَةً

إِلَيْكَ يَوْمَ الْقِيَامَةِ

Allahumma fa ayyumā mu'minin sababtuhu faj'al dhalika lahu qurbatan ilaika yawmal qiyamah

O' Allah! If I should ever abuse a believer, please let that be a means of bringing him near to You on the Day of Resurrection. (Sahih al-Bukhari 6361)

It is tough at times to think back of the inconsistencies and mistakes that we have made, particularly in dealing with other people. Some of these mistakes were made unknowingly, the consequence being the severity of the insult we made to others. Sometimes we are aware that we made a joke, comment, or sarcastic remark, or gave a look or glance to someone that upsets them. Perhaps they did not raise it with us because of their love, care, and respect for us. Perhaps, we may never see them again after that.

That does not change the fact that there is something owed to them from us, and this was something that our Prophet s.a.w. was very careful and cautious about. There is a chapter in Sahih Bukhari regarding the invocations of the Prophet s.a.w. on this matter. Imam al-Bukhari labelled this chapter as the one detailing the statement that if we should harm someone, let that be a means of purification and mercy for the person harmed.

The Prophet s.a.w. was the least likely of all of humanity to bring harm, difficulty, and rancour upon others, and yet we see that the Prophet s.a.w. was very worried and concerned about this matter as something in his spiritual connection to Allah s.w.t. What he would owe others in the rights they deserve between them, him and Allah. Let us study this *hadith*—how do we cure ourselves, how do we heal ourselves? From an insult that we have made to others. From something we have done to someone, the gravity and severity of which, we are unaware. It is not sufficient to merely say *astaghfirullah* multiple times or that we will never do it again. There is a *du'ā'* that was taught to us by the Prophet s.a.w in this regard. Abu Hurairah r.a. said, "I heard the Prophet s.a.w. make this invocation..",

اللَّهُمَّ

O' My Lord, only You can.

فَأَيُّمَا مُؤْمِنٍ سَبَبْتُهُ

O' Allah, any believer that I have insulted, any believer that I may have made *sabb*, abused, or wronged; anyone that I have made to feel small by me. Any believer that I have wronged, or I have cursed, or I have said something that has insulted them or hurt their feelings;

فَاجْعَلْ ذَلِكَ لَهُ قُرْبَـةً إِلَيْكَ يَوْمَ الْقِيَامَةِ

O' Allah, make the means of my abuse to them or my wronging to them, the reason that they are close to You on the Day of Judgement.

What a beautiful *hadith* of the Prophet s.a.w. What a compassionate and amazing human being our Prophet Muhammad s.a.w. was. Once again, "O' Allah, whichever believer that I have cursed, I have wronged. O' Allah make that cause of my ridicule of them or wrong or speaking ill of them in their presence or outside of their presence; O' Allah, make that something that draws them near to You on the Day of Judgement. Make that be something as a reward for them on the Day of Judgement, that Your nearness is provided to them."

If we are unacquainted with this *du'ā'* in its Arabic from or we have not been able to memorise it, may this book of Ramadan Therapy be an assistance to its memorisation and understanding. May Allah accept that from us as it was accepted from our Prophet Muhammad s.a.w., may Allah s.w.t. heal our hearts and make this Ramadan a therapy that can overcome that impulse of wronging others, of our sarcasm, of our putdown, our bullying, and our unfair treatment of others knowingly and unknowingly.

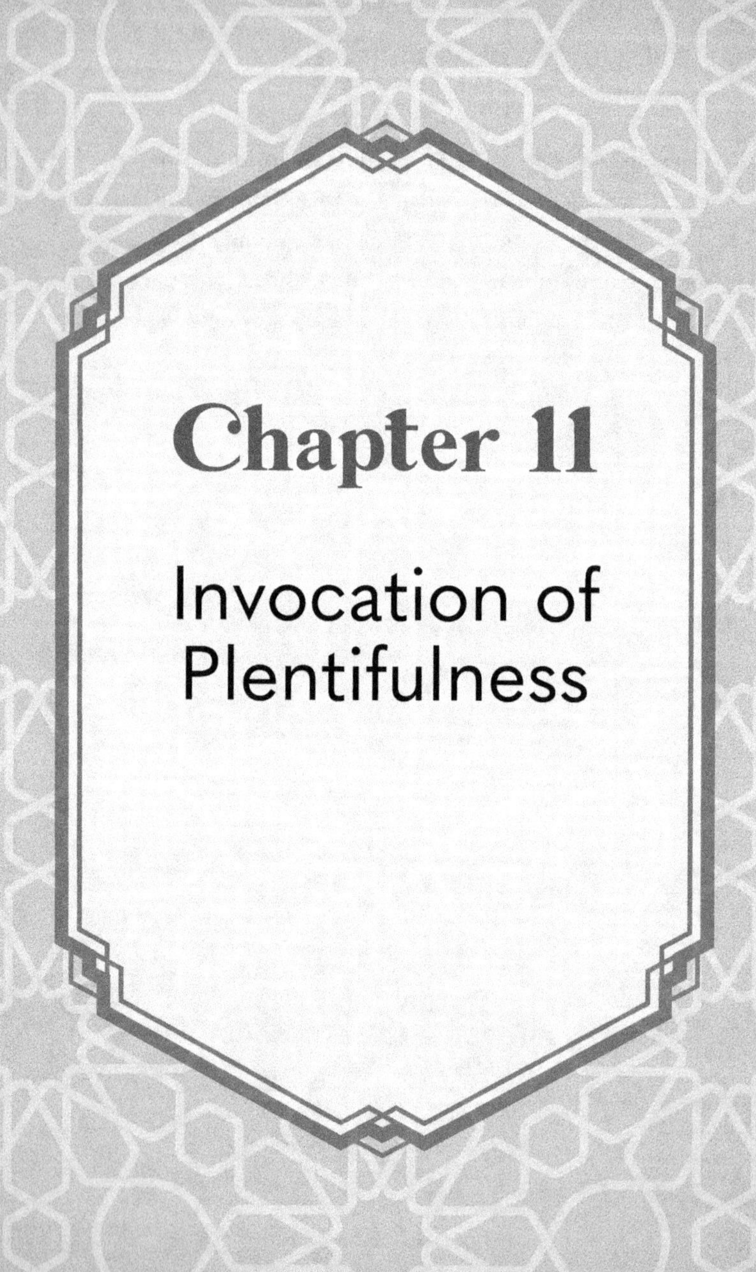

Chapter 11

Invocation of Plentifulness

لاَ إِلَهَ إِلاَّ اللَّهُ وَحْدَهُ لاَ شَرِيكَ لَهُ، لَهُ الْمُلْكُ، وَلَهُ الْحَمْدُ، وَهُوَ عَلَى كُلِّ شَيْءٍ قَدِيرٌ

Lā ilāha illallah waḥdahu lā sharīka lah, lahul-mulku wa lahul-ḥamd wa huwa 'alā kulli shayi'n qadīr.

None has the right to be worshipped but Allah, the One Who has no partners, to Him belongs Dominion and to Him belong all the Praises, and He has power over all things (i.e. Omnipotent). (Sahih Bukhari 3293)

This is a *hadith* is from the collection of Imam Malik, it is an authentic *hadith* and this statement of the Prophet s.a.w. is one of the most comprehensive and most used powerful *dhikr* and elevated form of asking Allah s.w.t. for His love, protection, healing, forgiveness, for the removal of our sins and for giving in charity.

Nevertheless, the root statement of this *du'ā'* is we will use it on the Day of Arafah, we use it when we are standing on as-Safa, we will use it when standing on the mountain of Marwa, we use it as we enter our city after a trip, it is a *du'ā'* that is used regularly in a repertoire of the invocation of the Prophet Muhammad s.a.w. Abu Hurairah r.a. reports that the Prophet s.a.w. said, "The one who says this one hundred times in his day…" Make it a habit to do this, it does not have to be all in one go, some can be in the morning, some can be in the afternoon, some can be in the evening, some can be after the prayers, it is a regular habit to make this plentiful.

لاَ إِلَـٰهَ إِلاَّ اللهُ وَحْدَهُ لاَ شَرِيكَ لَـهُ، لَـهُ الْمُلْكُ، وَلَـهُ الْحَمْـدُ، وَهُـوَ عَلَـى كُلِّ شَـىْءٍ قَدِيـرٌ

The one who says the *du'ā'* above a hundred times in their day, it is the equivalent of freeing ten slaves. Imagine that there are ten human beings whose lives and rights have been usurped, taken away, their power of decision on everything is removed from them; they have nothing in their own command, they are owned, beast of burden, and yet by us entering into their life, we gave them freedom. Ten human beings that we freed from bondage. A hundred times a day of the *du'ā'* above is equivalent to freeing ten souls from bondage.

Not just that, we are also given a hundred *hasanat*—blessings from Allah, and from our account a hundred sins are forgiven, expiated, and pardoned. The Prophet s.a.w. said the sins are wiped out, as if they never happened or existed.

It has been erased, expunged, and completely extinguished. This *du'ā'* will be his protective armour, his shield from the penetration and the assault of the *shaytān* throughout his day. *SubhanAllah*. Let's recount the blessing.

What does it give us?

1. Freed 10 slaves

2. Been given 100 blessings

3. Been freed from 100 sins, as if they were wiped out and never existed

4. Been given an armour, a protective shield from the influence, touch, harm of the *shaytān* until we retire in our bed at night

5. There is no one who will meet Allah on that day (Day of Judgement) who is better than the person who recites this *dhikr*, except for somebody who has said it more.

SubhanAllah. We ask Allah s.w.t. to protect us from our sins, to remove our sins, to elevate us with a hundred *hasanat*, to be from those of us that Allah blesses to give the freedom to ten slaves and the reward in that, to protect us from *shaytān*, our children, our family and our home, and no one is better than ourselves, except for those who recite this *du'ā'* more. *Allahumma āmīn*.

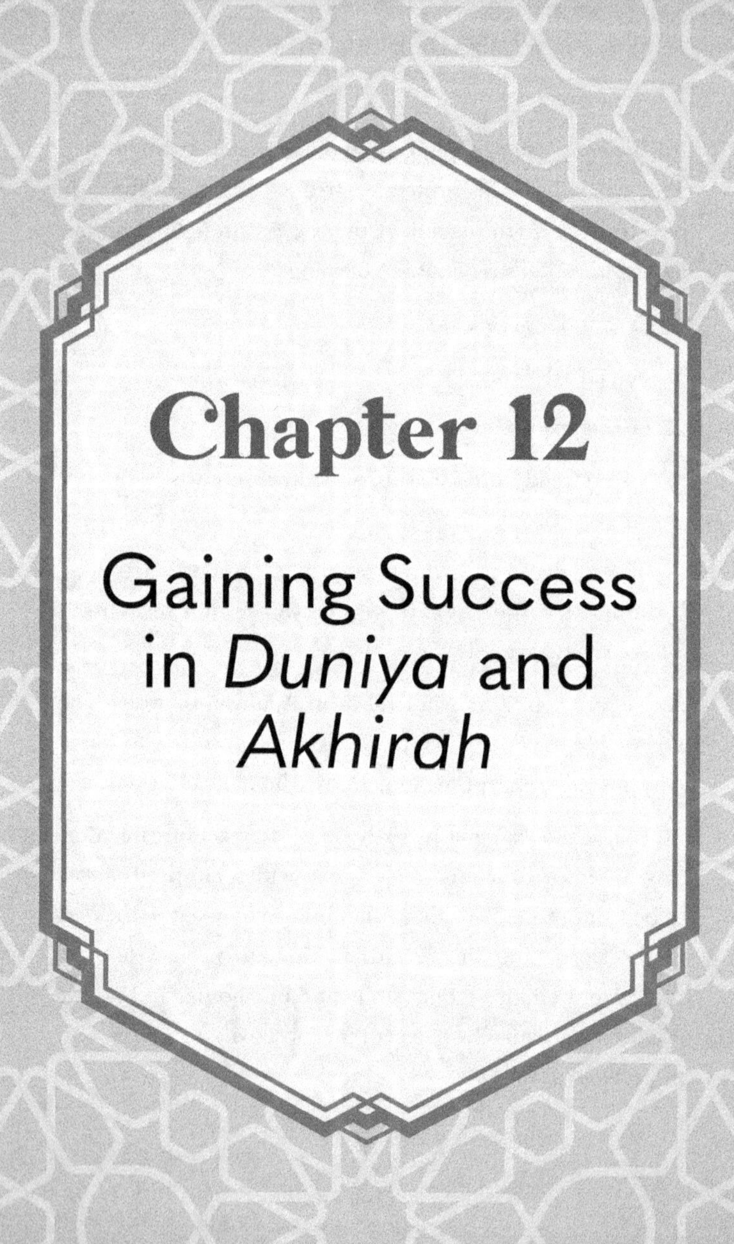

Chapter 12

Gaining Success in *Duniya* and *Akhirah*

رَبَّنَآ ءَاتِنَا فِى ٱلدُّنْيَا حَسَنَةً وَفِى ٱلْءَاخِرَةِ حَسَنَةً وَقِنَا عَذَابَ ٱلنَّارِ (٢٠١)

Rabbanā ā'tinā fid dunyā ḥasanatan wa fil ākhirati ḥasanatan waqinā 'adhāban-nār

Our Lord, give us good in this world and good in the Hereafter, and save us from the punishment of Fire. (al-Baqarah, 2:201)

This *hadith* is collected by Imam Bukhari, it is an authentic *hadith* narrated from Anas ibn Malik. A little background about Anas ibn Malik—he was a young child at the time the Prophet s.a.w. was in al-Madinah. When he was about eight or nine years old, his mother came to the Prophet s.a.w. and she said "O' Rasulullah, I want you to take my son, Anas, and use him as your personal assistant. He can do anything that you ask of him, *insha Allah*. Run your errands and so on." The Prophet s.a.w. understood that in her offerings, what she meant was, "I want you to teach him everything, I want him to be around you, I want him to be inside and outside."

And because Anas ibn Malik was young, he was able

to enter places that other people could not and to be with the Prophet in places that other people could not. Therefore, Anas ibn Malik was one of those *saḥābah* who has encyclopedic knowledge of the Prophet s.a.w.'s personal details, his personal rituals and habits that other *saḥābah* may not have seen. Anas ibn Malik lived to a very old age; one hundred years old. He was one of the final *saḥābah* to return to Allah s.w.t. and he left behind a wealth of information about the *sunnah* of the Prophet Muhammad s.a.w. This particular *du ʿā'*, he says, is a *du ʿā'* that we are all aware of, but we need to unpack it, contemplate, and reflect upon it.

$$\text{رَبَّنَآ ءَاتِنَا فِى ٱلدُّنْيَا حَسَنَةً وَفِى ٱلْءَاخِرَةِ حَسَنَةً}$$

$$\text{وَقِنَا عَذَابَ ٱلنَّارِ (٢٠١)}$$

(al-Baqarah, 2:201)

Anas ibn Malik said, "This is the most utilised *du ʿā'* of the Prophet s.a.w. that I witnessed." That does not negate the fact that there may be other *saḥābah* who used the same statement and narrate other *du ʿā'* of the Prophet s.a.w. However, because Anas was very close to the Prophet s.a.w., he had intimate details of the privacy of the Prophet s.a.w. and he could be with the Prophet s.a.w. at places where others could not which somewhat tells us that Anas r.a. is telling us something that was not just witnessed by him, but would not have been something of common knowledge.

The second thing that we take from this *hadith* is that the *ṣaḥābah* counted the *du ʿāʾ* of Prophet s.a.w., they were careful and would observe which ones he recited more. Therefore, Anas ibn Malik is mentioning this is as if he is preferring for us to make this *du ʿāʾ* regularly in our supplications to Allah. Third, we see that the *du ʿāʾ* which the Prophet s.a.w. made the most are those from the Qur'an, which sets a very important precedent for us to pay heed to the statements in the Qur'an where Allah commands the Prophet, by saying,

"And invoke me O' Muhammad, say in your prayers, 'O' my Lord, increase me in knowledge.'"

"Invoke me O' Muhammad, say: 'O' my Lord, I ask you to protect me from the impulses set upon me that have been set up by the *shāyaṭīn*.'"

"Invoke me and say, 'O' Allah, You are the Possessor of all the kingdoms, You give from this kingdom whom You will and You give honour, You take whom You will, You humiliate and bring to humiliation whom You will.'"

There are so many *du ʿāʾ* in the Qur'an that are phrased with Allah's instructions to the Prophet s.a.w. However, this *du ʿāʾ* of Prophet s.a.w. is taught and found in Surah al-Baqarah, in verse 201. This is where Allah s.w.t. says that there are some people who when we say to them—fear your

Lord, they rebel. Then there are others who, when they invoke God, they say, "O' my Lord, give us greatness in this *duniya*" and they forget the *akhirah*—they have very little to say about the next life. Then He says, but there are the righteous, the best of humanity who say:

$$\text{رَبَّنَآ ءَاتِنَا فِى ٱلدُّنْيَا حَسَنَةً}$$

Our Lord, give us something great in this *duniya*

$$\text{وَفِى ٱلْـَٔاخِرَةِ حَسَنَةً}$$

And Allah give us equal greatness in the *akhirah*. Therefore, we see this parity, that whatever we ask for the *duniya*, do not forget the *akhirah*. Do not forget our share in the *duniya* but make our *akhirah* a focus. For every *duʿāʾ* we make in the *duniya*, there must also be one good for the *akhirah*. For every good thing of the *duniya*, ask for something good of the *akhirah*. However, double it, and also ask for protection from what is found in the *akhirah*.

$$\text{وَقِنَا عَذَابَ ٱلنَّارِ (٢٠١)}$$

This is the third part of the *duʿāʾ*. "O' Allah save us from the torment of the hellfire." These are powerful statements. Three important *duʿāʾ*. "O' Allah give us good in this *duniya*. Give me good in this life and give me extra knowledge."

Therefore, when we refer to the *du'ā'* of knowledge in Surah Ta-Ha, "My Lord, increase me in knowledge." (Ta-Ha, 20:114), we remember the word of the Prophet s.a.w. where he said in a *hadith* of Muawiyah and Bukhari, "The one whom Allah wishes for him goodness in this world, they will be given by Allah an understanding of the faith." (Sahih Bukhari 71) Remember that it is not just the practice, but the understanding of it.

Therefore, when we are asking Allah to give us good things, remember that included within that *du'ā'* are all the other *du'ā'* that we are asking for. This is a comprehensive *du'ā'*. The Prophet s.a.w. taught that when it comes to the comprehensiveness of the *du'ā'* of the *duniya*, we should also specify things of the *akhirah*. Thus, when he says make *du'ā'* for Jannah, do not just make *du'ā'* for Jannah, but ask for al-Firdaus al-ula'. Ask for the highest level of Jannah which is Jannatul Firdaus; may we all be gathered there with our Prophet s.a.w.

Notice the word used is *hasanat*, it is translated as good, and *al-hasan* is distinguished from *al-qabīhah*. *Hasan* is the opposite of the word of ugliness, or sinfulness. When we use the word *hasan*, it is something that is of physical beauty. It is something of a physical relationship that is tangible. *Khayr* is more metaphorical, there is goodness in it. *Khayr* can be anything—it can be *khayr* in our heart, in our wealth and in our health. However, *hasanat* is something that we want, something that is tangible.

Abdullah ibn Abbas r.a. interpreted this *du'ā'* in Surah al-Baqarah, verse 201, that the *hasanat* involved in what the Prophet s.a.w. was invoking is to have a good spouse. To have a happy life with our family. Make this *niyyah* in our heart, "O' Allah make my wife my happiness in this life. O' Allah make my husband my happiness in this life. O' Allah complete me with them. Make them the treasure of my life. O' Allah, I am not yet married, O' Allah send me goodness in this *duniya*." That is what Abdullah ibn Abbas meant when he said that when we make this *du'ā'* and we are not married, we are asking Allah for a righteous spouse. This is one of the secret ways of asking Allah s.w.t. to send us goodness in our family and in our home, and if we have not yet built a house and built a family with others, ask Allah through this *du'ā'*. "O' Allah, make my family relationship a means for my success in the *akhirah* and protect us from the torment of the hellfire."

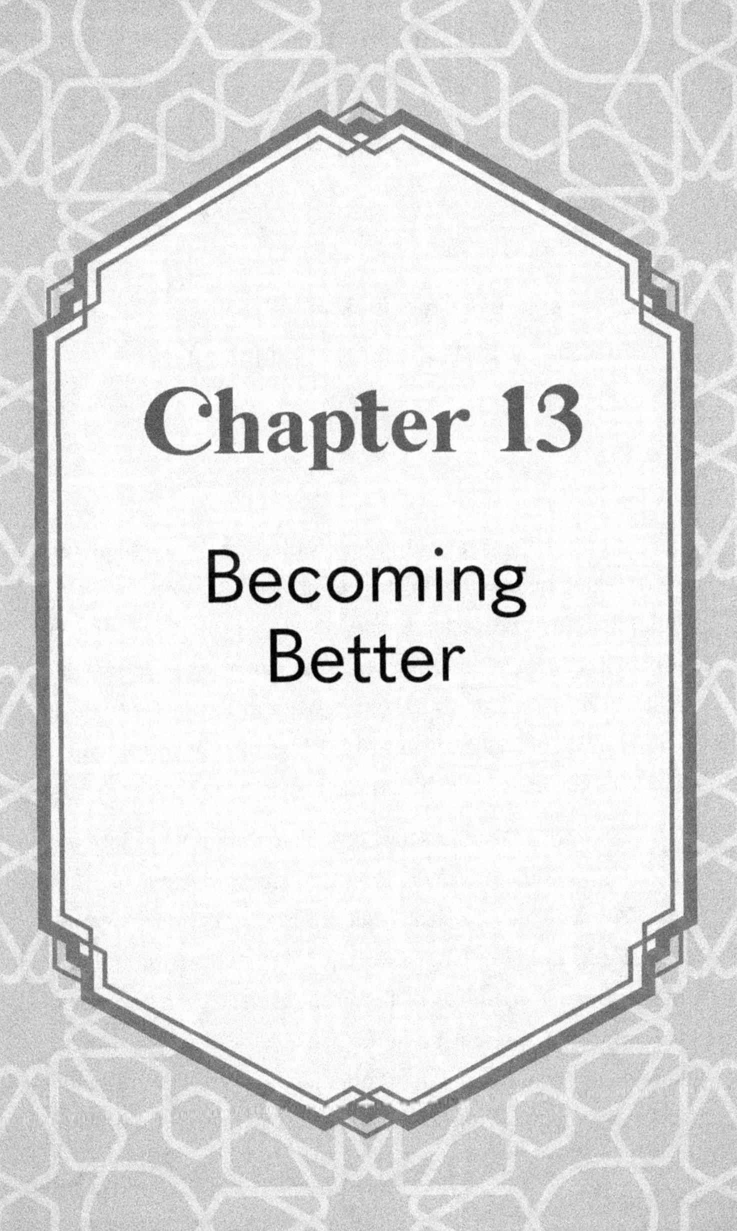

Chapter 13

Becoming Better

Ramadan Therapy

اللَّهُمَّ أَعِنِّي عَلَى ذِكْرِكَ وَشُكْرِكَ وَحُسْنِ عِبَادَتِكَ

Allahumma a' 'inni 'ala dhikrika wa shukrika wa husni 'ibādatika

O' Allah, help me in remembering You, in giving You thanks, and worshipping You well.
(Sunan Abi Dawud 1522)

This *du'ā'* was taught by the Prophet s.a.w. to one of the young people that he has chosen to be his ambassadors. This is a very powerful *hadith*. It was reported by Muadh ibn Jabl, from an authentic chain of narrators found in the collection of Imam Abu Dawud. Muadh ibn Jabl r.a was a young man, probably around 17-18 years of age at the time the Prophet s.a.w. gave him these instructions.

When the Prophet s.a.w. described Muadh ibn Jabl, he said that he is the most cognisant and knowledgeable of what is *halal* and what is *haram*; what is right and what is wrong. Equally, Muadh ibn Jabl r.a. was also a fierce warrior and one of the great companions of the Prophet s.a.w. even though he was young in age, but he had a great sense of discernment, knowledge, and the ability to understand. We will find many *hadith* where the Prophet s.a.w. would sit with Muadh and mentor him on each and every one of the said *hadith*.

One such *hadith* was when Muadh was sitting behind the Prophet s.a.w. on his camel mount. The Prophet s.a.w. would say, "O' Muadh, do you know what Allah demands of His servants?" and the Prophet went on to instruct him. There is a famous *hadith* of Muadh ibn Jabl in Sahih at-Tirmidhi where the Prophet s.a.w. taught him that the mastering of everything in life eventually came down to controlling of the tongue. "Shouldn't I tell you the thing that if you master it, you will have dominance over everything in your life?" and Prophet s.a.w. held out his tongue and pointed it to Muadh. Prophet s.a.w. then said, "I warn you of your tongue." On other occasion the Prophet s.a.w. said, "O' Muadh, I'm sending you to the people of Yemen, they are the people of scripture—Jews and Christians." This was the last time Muadh met the Prophet s.a.w and was also the Prophet's farewell advice to his companions. The Prophet s.a.w. had said to him, "I don't know if I will see you again."

Muadh ibn Jabl narrated that, "The Prophet took his hand and he interlaced it with mine. He held my hand in his hand. Our hands were together." Muadh did not want to let it go, so the Prophet s.a.w. began to walk with him. "He was walking with me to the outskirts of Madinah and he said, "I'm going to send you to the people of Yemen and you will call them to the *tawhid* of 'There is no God, but Allah'.

If they accept, teach them about *solah*, then if they accept, teach them *siyam*, then if they accept, teach them *zakat* and if they accept, inform them of *hajj*. Mentor them in their faith in God as I mentored you, O' Muadh."

Here then the Prophet s.a.w. said to Muadh, "O' Muadh, by my Lord, I love you. By Allah, I love you. Truly, I love you." Can we imagine the Prophet s.a.w. saying that to us? *SubhanAllah* if there is anything to be jealous of, something that was coveted, it would have been that Muadh garnered in the heart of Prophet s.a.w. It is as if this love was in the heart and mind of the Prophet s.a.w, so he was going to say something to Muadh, because of this love the Prophet s.a.w had for him. He said, "Muadh because of this love, I give you this legacy—this concise bit of important advice. I'm going to leave you with these words—don't ever let any of your prayers come to an end, except that at the end of the prayer, you say:

$$اللَّهُمَّ أَعِنِّيْ عَلَى ذِكْرِكَ وَشُكْرِكَ وَحُسْنِ عِبَادَتِكَ$$

'O' Allah, help me and allow me in my next prayer. Allow me further to remember You better and to show You greater gratitude and gratefulness. And to worship You in an ever more excellent manner.'"

In other words, "O' Allah, I want You to assist me and

help me to remember You and be in Your remembrance and to be more thankful and grateful to You O' Allah. And to be ever more excellent and pleasing to You through a proper service and worship of You, O' Allah." Let us analyse these important words.

First, after every prayer. The *'ulamā'* have disagreed as to what that means. Many of the *'ulamā'* held the opinion that it should be before we say *assalamualaikum* to our right then our left, meaning after we have made our *tahiyatul* then our *durood* upon the Prophet s.a.w. and Prophet Ibrahim. So before we say *salam* and while we make the other *du'ā'*, we say the *du'ā'* above. Other *'ulama* said that, it is after the *salam*. Meaning, after our *assalamualaikum* to the right and left, we then say the *du'ā'* above.

The Prophet s.a.w. mentioned it only once, but there are some *'ulamā'* who said that the Prophet s.a.w. habitually did things in his ritual prayers three times after the *solah*. If we are going to do it after the *solah*, seeing as how some have said that it is an exception, it is permissible in this case. There is an elevated reward for that. Imagine if the Prophet s.a.w. is before us and he tells us that he loves us and wants to teach us something. And this is the *du'ā'* he chose. This is the *du'ā'* he chose as he was sending a man far away from him to the people of Yemen because that is the pursuit that all of us are going through, especially for those of us who live as minorities.

Ramadan Therapy

We want Allah s.w.t. to accept this *du'a'* from us. It will bring healing and stability to our prayer. Therefore, if we are struggling with *solah*, this is the *du'a'* we make. If we are finding it difficult to concentrate, this is a *du'a'* to make. If we are finding it difficult to wake up for our *fajr*, make this a part of the *du'a'* that we make. "O' Allah, help me, I finished this prayer, but help me remember You more in the next one. To be thankful to You O' Allah, so that I can prostrate to You; we know You while others have forgotten You. That I remember You when others are distracted from You, O' Allah. And O' Allah, allow me to be evermore excellent and pleasing in my manner of worship of You. O' Allah make my *Zuhr* prayer great, but make my *Asr* prayer that is coming up even greater than my *Zuhr*. O' Allah make me of those who have benefited from this *solah*, but make my next *solah* even greater, O' Allah."

The final thought is that we should share our love with each other and if there is somebody whom we love, especially in this blessed month of Ramadan—whether our father, mother, brother, sister, wife or husband, son or daughter, let them know that we love them. The Prophet s.a.w. was never shy to use that word and he said to Muadh r.a. "By Allah, I love you, O' Muadh." May Allah s.w.t. make us the beloved of the Prophet s.a.w. and be near to him , which will allow us to join with Muadh ibn Jabl r.a. and our Prophet s.a.w. in the highest level of Firdaus.

Chapter 14

Protection from the Evil

Ramadan Therapy

Surah al-Ikhlas

بِسْمِ ٱللَّهِ ٱلرَّحْمَٰنِ ٱلرَّحِيمِ

قُلْ هُوَ ٱللَّهُ أَحَدٌ (١) ٱللَّهُ ٱلصَّمَدُ (٢)

لَمْ يَلِدْ وَلَمْ يُولَدْ (٣) وَلَمْ يَكُن لَّهُ كُفُوًا أَحَدٌ (٤)

Bismillahi ar Rahmānir Rahīm

Qul huwallahu ahad (1) Allahuṣṣamad (2) Lam yalid wa lam yulad (3) Wa lam ya kullahu kufuwan ahad (4)

In the name of Allah Most Gracious Most Merciful.

Say, "The truth is that Allah is One. (1) Allah is Besought of all, needing none. (2) He neither begot anyone, nor was He begotten. (3) And equal to Him has never been any one." (4)

Surah al-Falaq

بِسْمِ ٱللَّهِ ٱلرَّحْمَٰنِ ٱلرَّحِيمِ

قُلْ أَعُوذُ بِرَبِّ ٱلْفَلَقِ (١) مِن شَرِّ مَا خَلَقَ (٢) وَمِن شَرِّ غَاسِقٍ إِذَا وَقَبَ (٣) وَمِن شَرِّ ٱلنَّفَّٰثَٰتِ فِى ٱلْعُقَدِ (٤) وَمِن شَرِّ حَاسِدٍ إِذَا حَسَدَ (٥)

Bismillahi ar Rahmānir Rahīm

Qul a' 'udhu bi rabbil-falaq (1) Min sharri mā khalaq (2) Wa min sharri ghāsiqin idhā waqab (3) Wa min sharrin-naffā-thāti fil 'uqad (4) Wa min sharri ḥāsidin idhā ḥasad (5)

In the name of Allah Most Gracious Most Merciful.

Say, "I seek refuge with the Lord of the daybreak (1) From the evil of everything He has created, (2) And from the evil of the dark night when it penetrates, (3) And from the evil of the women who blow on the knots, (4) And from the evil of an envier when he envies. (5)

Ramadan Therapy

Surah an-Nās

بِسۡمِ ٱللَّهِ ٱلرَّحۡمَـٰنِ ٱلرَّحِيمِ

قُلۡ أَعُوذُ بِرَبِّ ٱلنَّاسِ (١) مَلِكِ ٱلنَّاسِ (٢) إِلَـٰهِ ٱلنَّاسِ (٣) مِن شَرِّ ٱلۡوَسۡوَاسِ ٱلۡخَنَّاسِ (٤) ٱلَّذِى يُوَسۡوِسُ فِى صُدُورِ ٱلنَّاسِ (٥) مِنَ ٱلۡجِنَّةِ وَٱلنَّاسِ (٦)

Bismillahi ar Rahmānir Rahīm

Qul a' 'udhu bi rabbin-nās (1) Malikinnās (2) Ilāhinnās (3) Min sharril was-wāsil khannās (4) A'lladhi yuwas wisu fī sudūrinnās (5) Minal jinnati wannās (6)

In the name of Allah Most Gracious Most Merciful.

Say, "I seek refuge with the Lord of mankind, (1) The King of mankind, (2) The God of mankind, (3) From the evil of the whisperer who withdraws (when Allah's name is pronounced), (4) The one who whispers in the hearts of people, (5) Whether from among the *Jinn* or Mankind (6)

(Sunan al-Tirmidhī 3575)

"

We are going to take three *surah* of the Qur'an that are incredibly important and are linked together chronologically in the Qur'an—they are the last three *surah* of the Qur'an. Surah al-Ikhlas, Surah al-Falaq and Surah an-Nas. The last two *surah* have a combined name which is *al-muawwizatain*—the two *surah* that we read to protect ourselves. *Al-muawwizatain*, means that these are the two surah through which I ask Allah for protection. There are many *hadith* on these two *surah*, on this great *du'a'* of the Prophet s.a.w.

The Prophet s.a.w. said, and this is narrated in many books of *hadith*, "The one who reads Surah al-Ikhlas and *al-muawwizatain (meaning Surah al-Falaq and Surah an-Nas)* before they sleep and when they wake up". Take note here that the Prophet s.a.w. normally said, "When you wake up, and then when you sleep." However, in this particular *hadith*, it is unique, it is *before* we sleep and when we wake up.

The Prophet s.a.w. is in fact making a prescription for us. He is writing a way of healing, a way of settling our heart of removing jealousy, protecting ourselves from anguish and having a restful sleep. One of the things that we need to do before we sleep is to recite Surah al-Ikhlas, Surah al-Falaq and Surah an-Nas three times before we sleep, with a *niyyah* which is intention of seeking the protection of Allah and seeking His healing and therapy for us. The Prophet s.a.w. said this will suffice us from all things. (Sunan at-Tirmidhī 3575)

Ramadan Therapy

This will be enough of a medicine, of a healing, of an increase in our *barakah*, enough of everything—if we did it with the intention of seeking Allah s.w.t. inwardly and outwardly. Surah al-Ikhlas, the Prophet s.a.w. said in an authentic *hadith*, "It is equal to one third of the Qur'an", (Sahih Bukhari 5013), which is powerful. This is because a third of the Qur'an is revolving around who Allah is and what Allah is to us. That is what the whole *surah* is about. "Say to them He is Allah, alone in His uniqueness. He is One and there is no one like Him." He is the One on whom we lean, and we rely upon. He has not been begotten and has not been introduced into this world—has not been created. There is nothing like Him s.w.t. Allah is the One, the Alone, the Unique in His Majesty s.w.t.

Both the *surah* of *al-muawwizatain* are really incredible and there are two important aspects. The first *surah*, Surah al-Falaq, is about physical needs. It is about things that people can do. Envy, hate, wrath, and anger of others—it is a cloak against these feelings of others. The other, Surah an-Nas, is about the power that Allah has given to other beings of the dominion. There is the spiritual aspect that we worry about, the feelings of the heart, and reciting Surah al-Falaq is for that. To blind the jealous eyes, to turn away the hearts from craving what we have and for Allah to give us protection in what we have been blessed with.

Surah an-Nas relates to the non-physical, the Lord of mankind. The Master of mankind. From what troubles man in their chest, of the unseen lurking devil who seeks to influence people with that which is *haram*. These two *surah* when combined with Surah al-Ikhlas, suffices us from everything. It removes doubts from the heart and upholds and solidifies our *tawhid* in Allah s.w.t if we contemplate and study it. The *surah* of *al-muawwizatain* relate to our interaction with other people, the *was-was* or (doubts) within ourselves and the envy of others towards us. Use them as a *ruqyah* for ourselves, our family, our children, our home. Study their meaning and implement it into our life and process.

Notice that the last two surah are linked together and they were used as a medicine by the Prophet s.a.w. as was prescribed to him by Jibril. In an authentic *hadith* narrated by Imam Bukhari and Muslim, the Prophet s.a.w was not feeling well. In his dream, the Prophet saw. Jibril speaking with the angels and they were deliberating as to what was wrong with him and he said that this was a touch that had come upon him and was evil. It was seeking to bring harm to him and how was he therefore to undo it? The angel Jibril then taught the Prophet s.a.w. to recite the surah *al-muawwizatain*.

It is a very real and present danger of other people craving towards what we have, that internal whispering, that internal doubt machine, that internal negation of that which is good, or that which makes us jealous of others, coveting what others possess and the envying of others, becoming greedy for the things that we should not be greedy of. Through the surah *al-muawwizatain*, we seek for Allah to protects us from the evil meanderings of the jinn, the unseen, nefarious forces and of the *shāyatīn* of humankind.

This protection exists to also help against what we know as the best friend who incites towards evil, who calls us to that which is wrong, who invites us towards committing sinfulness and lewdness. May Allah protect us from both levels of devilish behaviour. May Allah help us to be able make it a constant in our lives to recite *Āyatul Kursi*, the last two verses of Surah al-Baqarah and these last three *surah* of the Qur'an especially before we sleep and when we wake up. To put them together as a medicine and increase upon it with Surah al-Fātihah. May Allah give us an opening between us and our enemies. May this Ramadan be one of health and wealth therapies for us and may Allah give us many more like it.

Chapter 15

Obtaining Allah's Good Pleasure

سُـبْحَانَ اللهِ وَبِحَمْـدِهِ عَـدَدَ خَلْقِـهِ وَرِضَـا نَفْسِـهِ

وَزِنَـةَ عَرْشِـهِ وَمِـدَادَ كَلِمَاتِـهِ

Subḥān Allahi wa biḥamdihi ʿadada khalqihi wa riḍā nafsihi wa zinata ʿArshihi wa midāda kalimātihi (Recite x3)

Hallowed be Allah and praise is due to Him according to the number of His creation and according to the pleasure of His Self and according to the weight of His Throne and according to the ink (used in recording) words (for His Praise). (Sahih Muslim 2726)

This *hadith* and *duʿāʾ* was taught by the Prophet s.a.w. to his wife, and draws to our attention how much love and care we should have for our spouse. This is a *duʿāʾ* that Prophet s.a.w. handpicked and taught his wife—how not just to worship hard and long but also to worship smart, by using the right *duʿāʾ* for the right occasion. This *hadith* is by Juwairiyah ibn Harith, the mother of the believers. We call her the mother of the believers because Allah says in the Qur'an, "The wives of the Prophet s.a.w. are like unto you like your mothers." (Surah al-Ahzab, 33:6) This means that we have the same love, care, and support in our hearts for them and that would even exceed that towards our own mothers. They also have the sacred rights in that regard, whereby no man may marry the wives of the Prophet s.a.w. after his departure to Allah.

The Prophet s.a.w. would exit the home in the morning when it was time for *Fajr* prayer. He would leave his wife just as she was about to begin her *Fajr* prayers while she was in her place of worship at home (masjid).

This is an important point—that we should have a masjid in our home. The word masjid comes from the word that refers to the place of our *sujud*, the place where our forehead touches the ground frequently in our faithfulness and remembrance of Allah s.w.t. That is the concept of a masjid. Therefore, a wife's *masjid* is a place where she is concentrated and dedicated at home—it could be a corner in the bedroom, or a place in the home that has been dedicated and demarcated as the place of worshipp—the prayer mat is there, and that when it is time to pray, this is the place where the family habituates. It is our *mihrab*. The word *mihrab* comes from the word battle. Battle station, war —*harb*. The word *mihrab* is where we battle our soul for our very existence in the next life.

Mihrab is the place where we correct the mistakes of our

day, it is the place where we settle our affairs with Allah. It is a place that we wage jihad against our soul. The greatest jihad is against ourselves that we struggle and battle to make ourselves better. Therefore, the Prophet s.a.w's wife has her masjid at home and she said, "I sat there and I was about to pray my *solatul Fajr*." Then she said, "I sat in that place until he returned." She said that the Prophet s.a.w. returned after he has finished his *Dhuha* prayers in the forenoon.

Thus, she has been sitting there close to 3, 4, maybe even 5 hours. The Prophet s.a.w. asked her, "Have you remained sitting there upon the same condition, doing the same thing in your worship, your *dhikr*, in the same way that I have left you in the morning, and that you have not gotten up?" She was there, making her *du'ā*, reading the Qur'an, making her *dhikr*, sending her *salawat* in that same spot and she said, "Yes, O' Messenger of Allah." After he heard her respond, the Prophet s.a.w then said, "As for myself, I said four sentences—three times each, and if these were to be put on a scale against and compared to everything you did up to this time in your day, it would be heavier on my scale." Then the Prophet s.a.w. taught her and our *ummah* the following:-

سُبْحَانَ اللهِ وَبِحَمْدِهِ عَدَدَ خَلْقِهِ وَرِضَا نَفْسِهِ وَزِنَةَ عَرْشِهِ وَمِدَادَ كَلِمَاتِهِ

The Prophet s.a.w. said that the three repetitions of these four statements are greater in scale than what was done in her *dhikr*. What does this mean? Allah s.w.t. inspires us through the Prophet s.a.w. that there is a system or formulation of *du'ā'* for the right time and the right place. This is a *du'ā'* that we should make every morning and every evening.

سُبْحَانَ اللهِ وَبِحَمْدِهِ عَدَدَ خَلْقِهِ

This means that Allah is free from all imperfection; and to Him is owed all praises from beginning to end, as many times as the number of His creations. Glorious is Allah in His complete perfection and no imperfection. To Him belongs all of the praises and glorifications as many times as the number of His creations.

وَرِضَا نَفْسِهِ وَزِنَةَ عَرْشِهِ

"And I praise Him and I seek His glorification in accordance to what would earn me His good pleasure, what would earn me the *rida* of Allah. What would make Him pleased with me and what has been making Him s.w.t pleased. And I praise Allah, seeking His glorification, freeing Him from all imperfections, making praise of Him in His number of creations. In the number that will give Him satisfaction and pleasure in my mention of Him and equal to the weight of His *'Arsh*. In the amount that is equal to the weighing of the *'Arsh* of *Ar-Rahman*."

Everything that is created is minuscule in comparison to the *'Arsh* of *Ar-Rahman*; everything that is in the Heavens and the Earth occupies the same amount of space as the size of a ring that is thrown in the vast desert. Then the next Heaven, compared to the Heaven above it, which contains our Heaven and our existence in it is like that of a ring thrown into yet another desert. Multiply that seven times until we come to the *Kursi*. *Āyatul Kursi* is based on the magnificent *kursi* of *Ar-Rahman*. All of the Heavens and the Earth is like a ring compared to the *Kursi* of *Ar-Rahman*. The *Kursi* of Allah, that *Āyatul Kursi* is based on, is like a ring in its expansiveness and its smallness in comparison to the *'Arsh* of *Ar-Rahman*. Nothing is created more magnificent that the *'Arsh* of *Ar-Rahman*. Nothing rises above it other than Allah s.w.t. who is elevated from all ascription and imitation equal to the weighing and the beautification of the throne.

وَمِدَادَ كَلِمَاتِهِ

"And I praised Him and free Him from imperfection, thankful to Him in the number of His creation. In that which will bring upon His good pleasure. In that which is the weight of the beautiful creation of His *'Arsh*, and equal to the ink that may be used in recording His names. And what would increase His name in that it is being praised by all. And the equal to the ink that may be used in recording the word praised that I have just mentioned." *Allahu Akbar.* What a beautiful *du ʿāʾ*. What a beautiful way of increasing our value. Say this *du ʿāʾ* three times, at the time of *Dhuha* and in the evening.

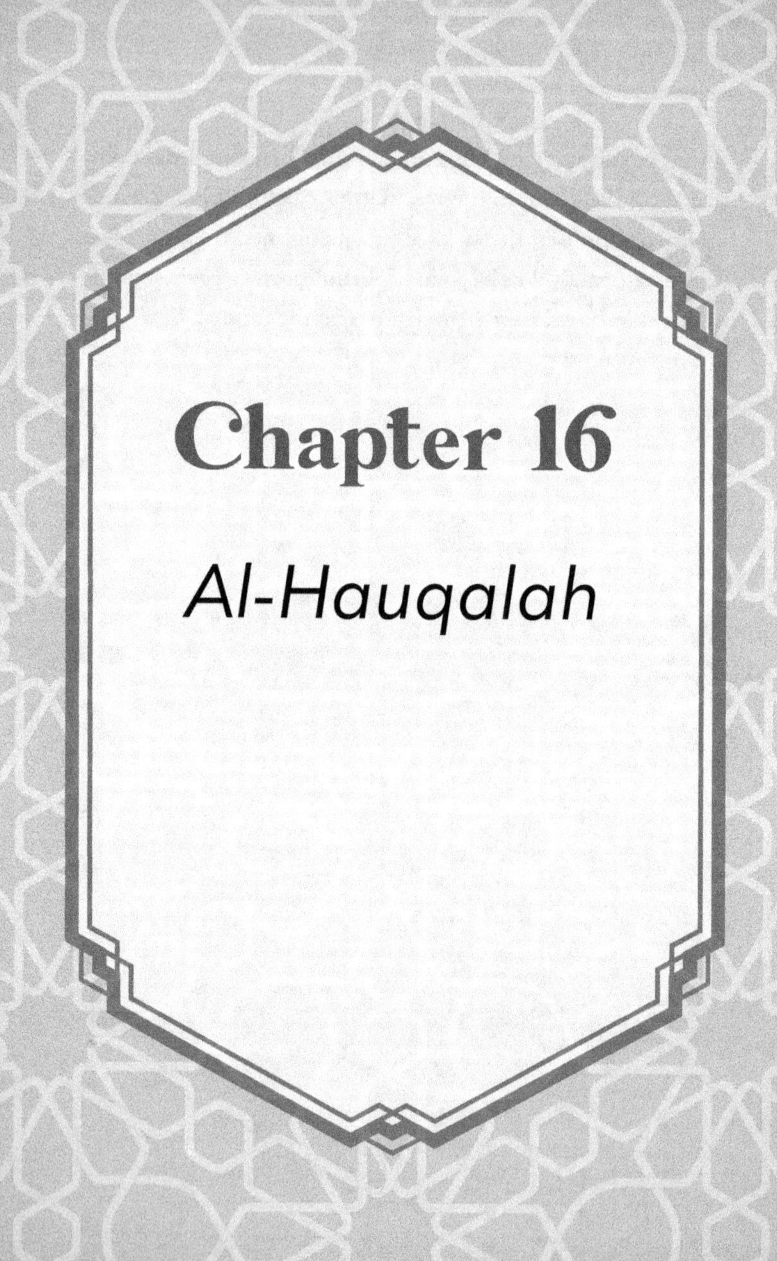

Chapter 16

Al-Hauqalah

لَا حَوْلَ وَلَا قُوَّةَ إِلَّا بِاللهِ

Lā haw la wa lā quwwata illā billah

There is no might or power except by Allah
(Sahih at-Tirmidhi 3601)

———◆———

This is one of the great *du'ā'*, one of the great *adhkar*—remembrances of the Prophet s.a.w. The *'ulamā'* called this *du'ā* 'al-hauqalah'. One of the most famous *hadith* about al-hauqalah is narrated in many books of the *sunan* and books of *hadith*. The Prophet s.a.w. was on a journey with some of the *sahābah*, and this *hadith* was narrated in the book of *tawhid* of Imam al-Bukhari.

In this *hadith* from Abi Said Abi Musa r.a., he narrated that they were travelling with the Prophet s.a.w, and on their journey whenever they ascended and climbed onto a hilltop or a mountain top, they would say *Allahu Akbar*. The Prophet s.a.w. said, "Confine your voices and do not trouble yourself too much and do not raise your voice so loud. Because the One you are invoking is not distant from you or unaware. He is not one who does not hear you or does not see you. He s.w.t is very near to you. You are in fact invoking Allah who is All-hearing, All-seeing and near to you."

Therefore we see that the Prophet s.a.w. admonishes us from elevating our voices excessively and unnecessarily when doing *dhikr*. It is a form of rebellion against Allah when someone goes to the extreme of yelling and raising their voice in *dhikr*, hopping around and doing all kinds of things at the same time. The Prophet s.a.w. said, "Your Lord is near you. He hears you, He sees you, He is close to you."

The Prophet s.a.w. then comes to Abdullah ibn Qaisin (who is actually Abi Musa who narrated this *hadith*) and says Abi Musa, "In myself, within myself, mere to myself, I was saying the *dhikr*, the *du'ā'* of Allah s.w.t. '*Lā haw la wa lā quwwata illā billah*', there is no might or power except by the leave and power given to us by Allah. There is no power, there is no ability, no way to turn or to move. No strength, no providence, except in that which Allah has provided. Whatever power I have, it is because of the power that Allah bestowed upon me."

Keep saying *al-hauqalah*, for verily that statement is a treasure from the treasures of paradise. *Al-hauqalah*, is a statement, it is an expression, first, of astonishment, a surprise at misfortune or a greatness that occurs. It should not be in use for one more than the other. It is not just in the moment of depression. *Al-hauqalah* should not only be used in situations like, "O' this is so sad, there is no power over our ability." In fact, it is a moment of rejoicing. Therefore, when we hear the *muadhin* call out *"Hayya alas solah, hayya alal falah"*—come to attention and alive to establish our prayer, come alive through our pursuit of success—our response is not to repeat what the *muadhin* said. In other parts of the *adhan*, we would repeat the *muadhin*. However, in this case, we say *Lā haw la wa lā quwwata illā billah*, meaning we can only rise up, we can only move, we can only answer this call with the might and power given to us by Allah s.w.t. Therefore, it is a moment of rejoicing, a moment of us acknowledging Allah. It is a moment of us standing before our Maker s.w.t., and keep in mind that every time we worship Allah, our *du'ā'* to Allah is something that brings us closer to Him. It does not have to be something that is expressed out loud.

An invocation is something that is within us and on our lips. It should just be in our heart that no one can hear it or that we cannot even hear it ourselves. The lips should move and the tongue should be wet. The Prophet s.a.w. said that one of the keys to opening the doors of Jannah is to let our tongue be wet from the excessive *dhikr* of Allah s.w.t.

Therefore, what are the specialties of this statement of *al-hauqalah*? In our mind, we need to have this mindset that we are calling Allah to grant us strength, might and power.

Ramadan Therapy

In our mind, it is to have the awareness that we know, at any time our might can be taken and deprived, and that Allah can alter our financial condition, our intellectual state, our financial resources. Know that Allah s.w.t. has promised to test us as mentioned in Surah al-Baqarah. This is the *du'ā'* that the *solihin* always made to prevent them from harm and it should be part of our daily repertoire of daily *du'ā'* to heal ourselves and protect ourselves against harm from befalling—which is our Ramadan Therapy. *Lā haw la wa lā quwwata illā billah*, "I have no might, no power except that which is possessed and given to me by Allah s.w.t."

We ask Allah s.w.t. to grant us the power and strength that we use in life. Connect this *hadith*, this *dhikr* with the statement of Allah, which is in a Hadith Qudsi authentically reported by Imam an-Nawawi, where the Prophet s.a.w. reports that Allah says, "Whenever a person draws close to Me, whenever My servants come close to Me, through the obligatory things that I have ordered, and then they begin to do the supererogatory—extra acts of devotion such as *al-hauqalah*, along with other *dhikr*, I become close to them and I befriend them so that I become the sight they see with, the hearing they hear with, and the strength they touch with." (Hadith Qudsi 25)

May Allah s.w.t. be the strength of our movement, the

sight of our eyes and the hearing of our ears. May Allah s.w.t. make the month of Ramadan a month of healing, therapy, recognition and reconciliation with others. May Allah s.w.t. open our hearts to each other.

Chapter 17

Supplication of *Laylatul Qadr*

اللّٰهُمَّ إِنَّكَ عَفُوٌّ تُحِبُّ الْعَفْوَ فَاعْفُ عَنِّي

Allahumma innaka ʿafuwwun tuhibbul ʿafwa faʿafu ʿannī

O' Allah, You are pardoning and You love to pardon, so pardon me. (Riyad as-Salihin 1195)

This is a *duʿā'* that is best when it is getting closer to *Laylatul Qadr*. It is best to memorise it, learn it and acquire the knowledge of it. It is a *duʿā'* that is preferred, prescribed, and taught to us by the Prophet s.a.w. as a healing and a blessing for our home and family and for our souls in this life and in the next, to be made for us and by us in *Laylatul Qadr*, the night of divine decree. Now this *hadith* is prescribed to the beloved wife of the Prophet s.a.w., the mother of the believers, ʿĀ'ishah bint Abu Bakr r.a.

ʿĀ'ishah was the nearest in affection to the Prophet s.a.w, may love, peace and blessings be upon her. In a *hadith* of Amr ibn Al-Aas, he said ʿĀ'ishah asked the Prophet s.a.w., "O' Messenger of Allah, if I was to come to certain knowledge that tonight is *Laylatul Qadr*, the night of the divine decree, what should I do during it?" This is the night when the Qur'an was first revealed. This night is greater than a thousand months—eighty-three years if we are to be literal.

The night where with the decree of Allah, peace is sought until the very last waking moment of the sun's rising. It is not just until we know *fajr* is near, and Allah uses that word, that the break of dawn has begun. Therefore, even up until the last second, we are encouraged through the understanding of this, to continue with our devotion, to continue to make our *du'ā'*. *Laylatul Qadr* is an auspicious occasion, upon which the knowledge as to which day it falls in particular, is withheld by the Prophet s.a.w. by the order of Allah s.w.t.

We do know that it has particular signs. It is in the last ten nights of the month of Ramadan, it is on an odd night, but that does not help with all the moon sighting that is happening. May Allah s.w.t. give us assistance, *Allahumma āmīn*. In fact, even before all the controversy of this sighting, the *'ulamā'* of the past always considered that once we go through the first half of the month of Ramadan, around the 16th or 17th night, that our thoughts should always be on *Laylatul Qadr*, so that every night comes alive. *Ahya Laylatul Qadr*. From the *sunnah* of the Prophet s.a.w., it was reported that he 'came to life' in the final ten days of the month of Ramadan.

Therefore, 'Ā'ishah said, "O' Messenger, just say, I have seen its signs and I've come to know, I felt that peace and I'm aware in my heart somehow, that Allah has inspired me. I have seen a dream for it..." These are all valid ways of measuring it for oneself. It is not something that we take from someone else and assume it is correct. Thus, let us just say that we see a dream that there is *khayr* on this particular night that is coming, and we inform our family, it does not necessarily mean that we are correct, but it is something that they can take action on, but at the same time do not miss out on any other night by saying that the dream had to be true, so pay attention to that.

The Prophet s.a.w. said, "If this feeling has come to you, then say, *Quli*. The word *Quli* means to repeat it often. It is not a one-off, but it is a consistent pattern of behaviour. Say:

اللّٰهُمَّ إِنَّكَ عَفُوٌّ

Say, "O' Allah, you are the One who pardons the most. You are the One who gives pardon." There is an explanation on the difference of *ghafur* and *'afuw*. O' Allah, You love to forgive by pardoning.

تُحِبُّ الْعَفْوَ

"You love to pardon. O' Allah, You are the Pardoner, and You love to pardon. O' Allah, You are the forgiving Pardoner, and You love to forgive and to pardon, so grant me forgiveness and pardon. Grant me freedom from my sin and my sinning."

Ramadan Therapy

We can translate the word *'afuw* in a number of ways. *'Afuw* means *'āfa,* that what is in the past is forgiven, pardoned, and will never be considered as if it happened. That is the most correct image and shadow of the word. That it is Allah who will deal with us, as if we have not committed that crime, not just to forgive it, but the crime is still present, its effect is still there. No, it is a pardon by Allah, that its effect is removed and our liability is also removed. Some of the *'ulamā'* postulated and said, "Well let's just say I have injured or harmed somebody else, how is it that I can be pardoned like I have never done that sin, when somebody to whom I owe a favour, I've done something wrong towards them?"

Al-Imam Ghazali in particular said, Allah will give that person whom we have wronged, such generosity, happiness and fulfillment in place of our error that they will forget the claim they have against us. *Allahu Akbar.* This is because our claim will still be there, but Allah's pardoning of us will not just be a benefit to us, but will be a benefit to the souls and the people that we have wronged, and therefore this *du'ā'* is a powerful healing therapy. O' slaves of Allah, make sure that this is the *du'ā'* that we fulfill throughout the next ten to thirteen nights of Ramadan. Do not take any risk. Make this a *du'ā'* that is in our days and in the evenings. Make sure that this is a *du'ā'* that is a part of our morning and evening routines. Make it plentiful that we do not forget it at other times.

"O' Allah, I recognise You alone are the One who is capable of pardoning without holding me ransom to my error." Nobody else will be able to pardon us in a way that it will be forgotten. Only Allah s.w.t. will pardon us, not forget, He will not forget, but He will overlook it with His compassion, His *'afuw* upon us. May Allah s.w.t. grant us the *'afuw* of *ar-Rahman ar-Rahim, al-Malik, al-Quds, as-Salam, al-Mukminun, al-Muhaiminun, al-'Aziz, al-Jabbar*. May Allah s.w.t. grant us *'afuw* of the *al-'Afuw*. Allah is the Only One who is capable of pardoning and not holding us accountable for what we have done in error. The only reason for that is because You s.w.t love to show this clemency, this pardon and this forgiveness that nobody else possesses.

Nobody else has that power, so Allah grant us pardon. Notice this *du'a'* is not a communal *du'a'*. We can make the *du'a'* with others and says *Fa'fu anna*—forgive us, but when the Prophet s.a.w. taught it to 'A'ishah, *fa'fuanni*, all of the narrations have it in a singular voice, meaning that this is something personal to us. We know our mistakes and we know the things for which we have fallen off the path. Therefore, take it seriously, do not make this as something that we are just in the *jamaah*, or praying *witr* and the imam says *fa'fuanna* and it is just a simple *āmīn*. No, this needs to resonate from the bottom of our gut, the depth of our soul, seeking the pardon of Allah s.w.t.

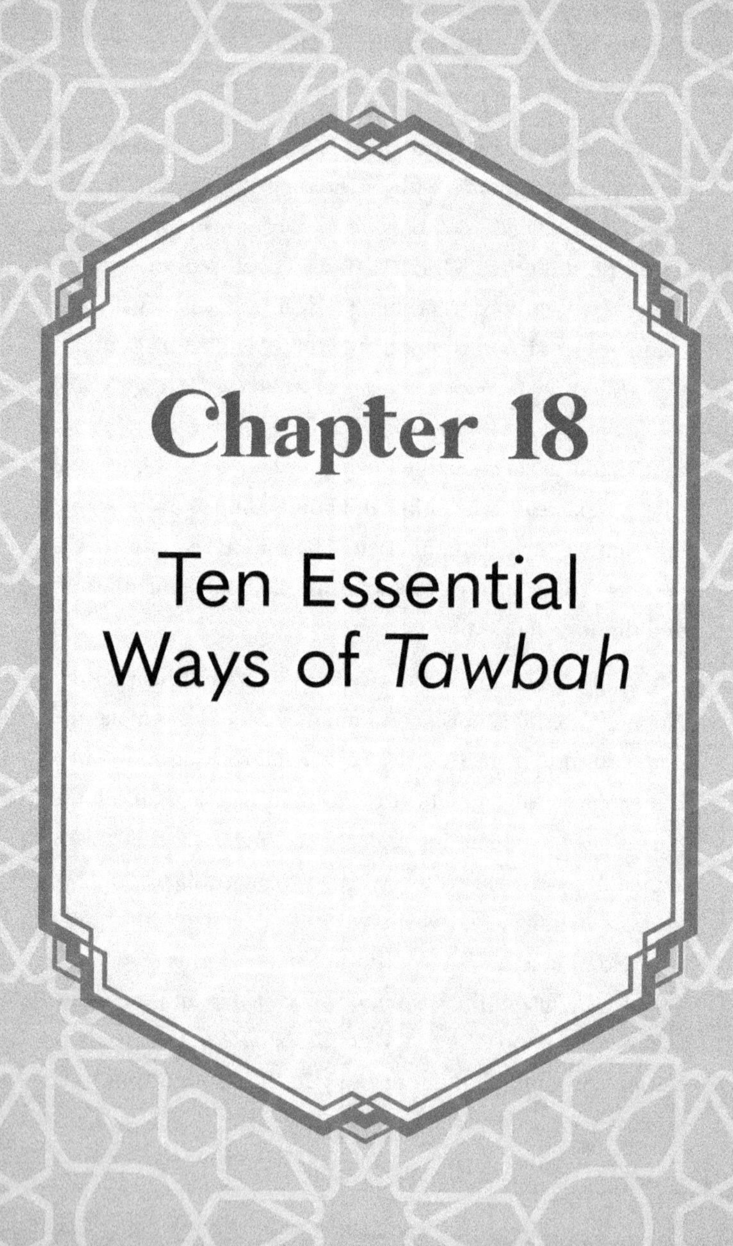

Chapter 18

Ten Essential Ways of *Tawbah*

حَدَّثَنَا مُسَدَّدٌ، حَدَّثَنَا أَبُو عَوَانَةَ، عَنْ عُثْمَانَ بْنِ الْمُغِيرَةِ الثَّقَفِيِّ، عَنْ عَلِيِّ بْنِ رَبِيعَةَ الْأَسَدِيِّ، عَنْ أَسْمَاءَ بْنِ الْحَكَمِ الْفَزَارِيِّ، قَالَ سَمِعْتُ عَلِيًّا، - رَضِي اللَّهُ عَنْهُ - يَقُولُ كُنْتُ رَجُلاً إِذَا سَمِعْتُ مِنْ رَسُولِ اللهِ صلى الله عليه وسلم حَدِيثًا نَفَعَنِي اللَّهُ مِنْهُ بِمَا شَاءَ أَنْ يَنْفَعَنِي وَإِذَا حَدَّثَنِي أَحَدٌ مِنْ أَصْحَابِهِ اسْتَحْلَفْتُهُ فَإِذَا حَلَفَ لِي صَدَّقْتُهُ قَالَ وَحَدَّثَنِي أَبُو بَكْرٍ وَصَدَقَ أَبُو بَكْرٍ - رضى الله عنه - أَنَّهُ قَالَ سَمِعْتُ رَسُولَ اللَّهِ صلى الله عليه وسلم يَقُولُ » مَا مِنْ عَبْدٍ يُذْنِبُ ذَنْبًا فَيُحْسِنُ الطُّهُورَ ثُمَّ يَقُومُ فَيُصَلِّي رَكْعَتَيْنِ ثُمَّ يَسْتَغْفِرُ اللهَ إِلاَّ غَفَرَ اللَّهُ لَهُ « . ثُمَّ قَرَأَ هَذِهِ الآيَةَ { وَالَّذِينَ إِذَا فَعَلُوا فَاحِشَةً أَوْ ظَلَمُوا أَنْفُسَهُمْ ذَكَرُوا اللَّهَ } إِلَى آخِرِ الآيَةِ .

Ramadan Therapy

Narrated Abu Bakr as-Siddiq:

Asma' bint al-Hakam said: I heard Ali say: I was a man; when I heard a tradition from the Messenger of Allah s.a.w., Allah benefited me with it as much as He willed. But when some one of his companions narrated a tradition to me, I adjured him. When he took an oath, I testified him.

Abu Bakr narrated to me a tradition, and Abu Bakr narrated truthfully. He said: I heard the apostle of Allah s.a.w. saying: When a servant (of Allah) commits a sin, and he performs ablution well, and then stands and prays two rak'ahs, and asks pardon of Allah, Allah pardons him. He then recited this verse: "And those who, when they commit indecency or wrong their souls, remember Allah" (Al-Qur'an 3:135). (Sunan Abi Dawud 1521)

This is a particular *hadith* of the Prophet s.a.w. that is foundational. The Prophet s.a.w. said, and this is in our pursuit of *tawbah*, our reform, return to Allah. The word *tawbah* means to return from the place that we should not have been, to return back to the path that we know is the right path, and it is a very important process in the life of every believer. Whenever Allah speaks about *tawbah*, He speaks about those who have believed, not those who are criminals.

In a Sahih hadith recorded by Imam Abu Dawud, at-Tirmidhi, the Prophet s.a.w said, "There is not an individual who commits a sin then after recognising the error of their ways, they stand up, and then they make a ritual purification, they make *wudū'*, and then prays and in one of the narrations it says two *rakaat*, two prostrations. They make *wudū'*, a good *wudū'*, in one narration that they make a really good *wudū'*, they are concentrating in it, they do the *duʿā'* of it and they make the *wudū'* and they pray two *rakaat* to Allah s.w.t. Then in the prayer and after the prayer, they ask Allah for forgiveness, except that Allah will forgive him." (Sunan Abi Dawud 1521)

Let us recount the ten ways that we can seek and pray that our errors are forgiven by Allah through a process of *tawbah* through a process of actively seeking to do something good for us. These ten are taken from Shaykh al-Sami ibn

Taimiyyah from his *fatawa*. He says:

1. State the crime or sin that we have done in our *du'ā'* to Allah and asking for it to be forgiven. Then, we make repentance for it, while seeking Allah's pardon; knowing in our heart what it was that was wrong, acknowledging it before Allah. Admit that we have wronged our own self. It is not somebody else, it is me. Understand that the actions that we have taken, has ruined our place with You, O' Allah and we want You; we ask You, we beg You to return us to a place of good with You, O' Allah.

2. Ask Allah for *istighfar* for the things that we know and the things we do not know. O' Allah, forgive us for what we know and what we do not know. *Istighfar* can be said by simply saying *astaghfirullah* multiple times, with the tongue, while in our heart is repentance and regret on what we know we have done wrong and the things we know have been done, but we cannot recount them. We are unsure which ones and how many.

3. Do good deeds. We do not know anything that can correct the behaviour of someone who has wronged people in their life, or those to whom we can no longer make it up to, as perhaps they have passed away. We have insulted someone with our words and now they have passed away. Years later we are regretful. We

cannot go and apologise to them. Therefore, what can we do? We can do a massive amount of good deeds that can overwhelm what is in our record. This is because Allah s.w.t. says, "Sinful deeds are wiped away, washed over with the good deeds that come after them."

4. Have our brothers, sisters, friends, and family make *du'ā'* for us. These people are people who think of us well, so they ask Allah for our forgiveness too. Somebody who is going to *hajj*, somebody who is going to *umrah*, somebody who is fasting, somebody we fed, somebody we gave a loan to, someone we were generous to, someone we smiled, and we make them feel better—we should ask Allah that they make *du'ā'* for us, because the *du'ā'* of a believer for his friend without them knowing is answered by Allah. Therefore, be regular in asking people to remember us well and speak well of us. Prophet Ibrahim a.s. made the *du'ā'*, "O' Allah, make my mention amongst the righteous, plentiful in the days to come" and that is why we remember him in our *ṣolah* and send the *salawat* upon him.

5. Give presents or gift to someone. When we do this, do it for the right reason and in the pursuit of pleasing Allah s.w.t. and therefore, it is encouraged to give gifts to others, it builds love between us and other people and it adds favour in other people's hearts that when we

give someone, they say *jazakallahukhayr*. We might think that it is not a powerful *du'ā'*, but it is. May Allah reward us with *khayr*. May Allah reward us with good. Perhaps that good is what turning us away from the errors that we have been performing and giving us assistance to go past it.

6. We also ask Allah to turn the hearts of people so that they gift us with acts of reward. That they give us something of the righteous deeds. That someone gives *sadaqah* or charity in our name. Someone remembers us in our life and after our death, makes *du'ā'* for us or does endowment for us or build a well that they share with us and feeds people on our behalf.

7. Grow closer to the Prophet s.a.w in order to gain his *shafaat* by following his *sunnah*, by modelling ourselves after him, by making mention of him. This is because the one that we mentioned, will mention us. The one that we loved, will love us. The one that we cared for, will care for us. The one whom we followed, will be our leader on the Day of Judgement. Hence, hope for the intercession and the *shafaat* of Prophet Muhammad s.a.w.

8. Relish the calamities that are sent to us by Allah as opportunities for us to display patience, so Allah reforms things in our life. When something bad happens, react

to it in a good way. Something that we are not happy about, something that we are disappointed in, say, "This was decreed by Allah and what He willed has occurred." Say, "I have no power, no might, no ability, except for what is given and granted by Allah. I can only do what Allah has strengthened me to do." Bear with strength the calamities and tests that are written for all of us. Some that are publicly seen, so we know that that person has been tested with illness or poverty or debt. However, others are internal that nobody knows of, such as having hardship with the family, wayward children, and many more.

9. Ask Allah s.w.t. to make us among those who, on the Day of Judgement are safe from His torment and punishment; but know that this is a way of expiating our sins. This is because Allah s.w.t. will test us on the Day of Judgement, and we ask Allah to give us relief and let us be from the seven categories of people who will be sheltered by Allah on that Day. Among the categories are a just governor, somebody who does their job well, someone who looks after the employees, their household, family and their society, somebody who is a good imam, somebody who is a good political leader, someone who does their job to the best of his/her ability, and a young person who grew up worshipping Allah into their old

age. Investigate these seven categories and see which one of them you can fit it into. (Riyad as-Salihin 449)

Ask Allah to show us His mercy and be regular in seeking His Mercy. Be plentiful in asking Allah for His pardon, for His forgiveness. Be plentiful in making our *istighfar*; multiple and plentiful times in our day and in our life.

10. Know that Allah s.w.t. has promised us, that if we are vigilant in our prayer and if we come to Him having completed them with good intention, in the best of our ability, then everything else in our life will be accepted. If our prayer is right, everything else will be accepted, even if there are omissions, sins, and mistakes along the way. Therefore, find solace in our *solah*, make it the *qurratul a'yun*, a coolness and a fresh breath of air in our life. Be regular in our commitment to the five essential daily prayers and the one that we forgot, the one that we missed, make it up. Make it up, as best as we can.

We ask Allah s.w.t. to teach us to turn to Him always, make a good *wudū'*, two *rakaat* and ask Him for His forgiveness whenever we have erred.

Chapter 19

Sincerity in Intentions

رَبَّنَا تَقَبَّلْ مِنَّآ إِنَّكَ أَنتَ ٱلسَّمِيعُ ٱلۡعَلِيمُ (١٢٧)

Rabbanā taqabbal minnā innaka a'ntas-samī-'ul 'alīm

Our Lord accept (this service) from us! Indeed, You—and You alone—are the All-Hearing, the All-Knowing! (al-Baqarah, 2:127)

◆

This *du'ā'* is from the Qur'an. It is a beautiful *du'ā'* from Surah al-Baqarah. Whenever we have *du'ā'* from the Qur'an, it is always important to know the context of the *du'ā'*. This *du'ā'* is found in Surah al-Baqarah, verse 127 and this is contained in the *du'ā'* of Ibrahim a.s. and Ismail a.s. as they were working together in the building of the Kaabah. This *du'ā'* is also mentioned by Imam Bukhari in the authentic *hadith* in the chapter of the Prophets. (Sahih Bukhari 3365)

In the chapter of the Prophets, it is about the statement of Allah s.w.t. in Surah al-Baqarah where Allah s.w.t. revealed to Ibrahim a.s. the command to build the Kaabah. Ibrahim a.s. and Ismail a.s. then began to build the House of Allah. Ibrahim a.s. was standing at *maqam* Ibrahim and Ismail a.s. was passing him rocks as they built on the foundation of the Kaabah. As the Kaabah grew higher and higher in elevation, they would recite the following every time they placed a rock:

$$رَبَّنَا تَقَبَّلْ مِنَّآ إِنَّكَ أَنتَ ٱلسَّمِيعُ ٱلْعَلِيمُ$$

"O' our Lord, accept this service from us. O' Allah accept this action from us, this intention from us, You are the one who Hears and Knows."

Starting from now, within our heart, our life, our being and our consciousness, make it a constitution of our life that anything that we do in our life—the worship of Allah, *siyam*, or whether it is the *zakat* that we have given, the *hajj* that we are performing, the *tawaf* we are making, whether it is just sitting on our bed and contemplating the creation of Allah, say the *du'a'* above. O' Allah, accept this from us. You are the One who hears what we have said and You are the One who knows what we are doing.

Let us have a thorough explanation of this *du'a'*. First, notice that it begins with "*Rabbana*". It is the plural word of saying *Rabbi*, my Lord. It is not just for 'me', but it is for everybody around us. Sometimes we are in our home, we have just finished our *solah* and our wife is busy in the kitchen. Our children are doing their homework, but as we sit with Allah s.w.t., do not sit there and say "*Rabbi*; My Lord alone." Remember them all. This was the habit of Prophet

Ibrahim a.s as mentioned in the *du'a'* above and in various other *du'a'* that he made.

This is an example of Ibrahim a.s., Nuh a.s. and other prophets—that they would join others in their collective *du'a'*, *Rabbana*, our Lord, all of us, those who believe in You and those who do not. In fact in Surah Ibrahim, Prophet Ibrahim a.s said, "O' Allah, for the one who disobeys me and won't believe in what You have sent to me, You are the Most Forgiving, I leave them to You, O' Allah." (Surah Ibrahim, 14:36) Remember to always have good in our *du'a'* for others.

Yet, there is the word "accept" in the *du'a'* above. Why "accept"? This is because there are many actions that we do that are *not* accepted by Allah s.w.t. May Allah s.w.t. protect us from this. Either because there is a problem with our *niyyah*, in our formality of it or how we functioned/purposed it. And yet even then, the people who lead us in prayer usually at the end of the prayer, in the *solatul tarawih* for example, in their *du'a'*, will say (or at least we hope that they will remember to say), "O' Allah accept from us what we have recited, and for whatever we made of mistakes, we ask You O' Allah s.w.t. to pardon us for it. O' Allah accept from us the month of Ramadan. Accept from us our fasting." The *sahabah* for six months after the month of Ramadan, they would say, "O' Allah, accept the month of Ramadan from us."

Therefore, in the constitution of a believer, the first lesson would be to recite the *du'ā'* above for everyone. The Prophet s.a.w. gave us a warning in an authentic *hadith*, where he said, "Perhaps a man would stand up and pray. At the end of the prayer, all that is written for him, for some of them at the end of the prayer, only half of its reward will be written, for others a quarter, for others even a tenth." May Allah protect us. Imagine having stood up and prayed, and receiving only a tenth of the reward. For other people, they are fasting all day, at the end of it, they gained nothing, except hunger and thirst as narrated in an authentic *hadith* (Sunan Ibn Majah 1371). May Allah protect us from the ones who do not control their tongues and act upon falsehood and false testimony. Allah is in no need of them to leave off their food and drink. May Allah protect us from such a state. Therefore, ask Allah to *accept* our deeds. It is as important as having to fulfill the deeds.

$$إِنَّكَ أَنتَ ٱلسَّمِيعُ ٱلْعَلِيمُ (١٢٧)$$

Allah, You alone O' Allah. You, only You are the All-Hearing. We say The-All Hearing because our presumption is that Allah sees us and hears us in any condition. Allah is nearer to His servants than our own jugular vein. He is not with us in our particular location, but He is transcendent from His creation, beyond comparison. He is not confined to this space that has been created by Him s.w.t. However,

His knowledge, hearing, and understanding of our condition are here. He has knowledge of what we will be, what has been, what has been willed and even though it could never happen, because we have made an alternate choice. He also knows what other choices we would have arrived at.

He is the All-Hearing of what is in the heart. He knows what the eyes may try to hide and are unable to see and are still buried in the chest of a man. Allah s.w.t. knows what is hidden. Not just what is in our chest, but what has not yet come to our mind and our chest; what we had not yet thought about. He knows what we will think before we even thought of it, what we intend before we intended it. His knowledge extends beyond what we have done to what we will do, to what we have done or what we could do. He knows what was, what is, what will be and what could be, even though it will never come to being, because He has not given it its ability to come to being, but what its outcome would have been is in His knowledge.

Therefore, this *du'ā'* is a powerful *du'ā'*. It is a *du'ā'* that builds sincerity between us. It is the *du'ā'* of Prophet Ibrahim a.s as he stood building the Kaabah. It is the *du'ā'* of the *anbiya*, the *du'ā'* of the *solihin*, the *du'ā'* of our Prophet Muhammad s.a.w. in following the footsteps of Ibrahim a.s. Make sure today, be plentiful with correcting your intentions by saying the *du'ā'* above.

Chapter 20

Duʿāʾ of Light

اللَّهُمَّ اجْعَلْ فِي قَلْبِي نُورًا وَفِي بَصَرِي نُورًا وَفِي سَمْعِي نُورًا وَعَنْ يَمِينِي نُورًا وَعَنْ يَسَارِي نُورًا وَفَوْقِي نُورًا وَتَحْتِي نُورًا وَأَمَامِي نُورًا وَخَلْفِي نُورًا وَعَظِّمْ لِي نُورًا

Allahummaj'al fī qalbī nūran wa fī basarī nūran wa fī sam'ī nūran wa'an yamīnī nūran wa'an yasārī nūran wa fauqī nūran wa tahtī nūran wa amāmī nūran wa khalfī nūran wa'azim lī nūran

O' Allah, place light in my heart, light in my sight, light in my hearing, light on my right hand, light on my left hand, light above me, light below me, light in front of me, light behind me, and enhance light for me. (Sahih Muslim 763)

This *hadith* is in Sahih Muslim and the *du'ā'* that is contained in it is such a beautiful *du'ā'*. It is the *du'ā'* of the Prophet s.a.w. that he would use when he would wake up to worship Allah while others were asleep. The person who witnessed the Prophet s.a.w making this *du'ā'* was one of the key narrators, Abdullah ibn Abbas r.a. He was a young man and he used to have access to the Prophet s.a.w because he was related to the Messenger s.a.w. and would stay over in his home.

In *Kitab al-Solah* in Imam Muslim, Abdullah ibn Abbas reported that the Prophet s.a.w got up from sleep and went to his water vessel, took out some of its water and he made *wudū'*. The Prophet s.a.w did not take out too much water that nothing was left behind and he did not take too little an amount of water that he did not have a good *wudū'*. This reminds us of the importance of being very careful, by not exaggerating in making *wudū'* with too much water. That even if we are in the middle of the river, do not waste water.

There is a *Riwāyah* narrated in Sunan Abi Dawud in this regard, and even though there is a bit of an issue with its chain of narration, its meaning is correct. Kuraib reported that Abdullah ibn Abbas r.a. spent a night in the house of the Prophet Muhammad s.a.w. and he said: the Prophet Muhammad s.a.w. made this *wudū'*. In this mention is also made (of the fact) that on that night the Prophet Muhammad s.a.w. made supplication before Allah in nineteen words. Kuraib reported: "I remember twelve words out of these, but have forgotten the rest."

This shows us the honesty of reporters of the *hadith*. He said, "Listen, there were nineteen different *du'ā'* that the Prophet s.a.w made, but I only remember twelve of them and forgot the others. May Allah forgive me." It is very important to be very careful of what we narrate from the Prophet s.a.w. In a *hadith* of 'Ā'ishah r.a., in Sahih Muslim, the Prophet s.a.w. said, "Let the one who misspeaks about me, in a way that I say something that I did not say, let them prepare for a seat in hellfire." (Sahih Bukhari 107) May Allah protect us from this. If there is a weak narration, we say that it is weak. If it is not from the word of Prophet s.a.w., do not attribute it to him. But these words are known as for being the words of the *du'ā'* of Prophet s.a.w. in the authentic Sahih of Imam Muslim. What are they? May Allah give us healing. Some of the most beautiful statements of the Prophet s.a.w., he begins by saying:

$$\text{اَللّٰهُمَّ اجْعَلْ فِىْ قَلْبِىْ نُوْرًا}$$

O' Allah, place for me, in my heart, *nūr*—light.

$$\text{وَفِي بَصَرِي نُوْرًا}$$

And in my sight, light.

وَّفِىْ سَمْعِىْ نُوْرًا

And in my hearing, light.

وَعَنْ يَمِينِي نُورًا

And on my right hand, light.

وَعَنْ يَسَارِي نُورًا

And on my left hand, light.

وَفَوْقِي نُورًا

And place light above me,

وَتَحْتِي نُورًا

and place light below me.

وَأَمَامِي نُورًا

And from in front of me, before me, let there be light.

وَخَلْفِي نُورًا

And from the back of me, let there be light.

وَعَظِّمْ لِي نُورًا

And O' Allah, grant me an abundance of light.

What a beautiful *hadith*. The context of light is very important. Whenever we speak about light in Islam, it is always in the singular. It is not plural light—*anwār*. Therefore, the Prophet repeated the same *du'ā'* by asking for the same light. That light is the light of guidance. The Prophet s.a.w. is saying, "O' Allah let my heart choose Your guidance. Let my heart see what my eyes fail to see. Let my hearing only be receptive to that which is pleasing to You. Let my sight only fall upon that which is pleasing to You. Let there be light above me, make guidance shroud me from above, from beneath from the right and from the left. O' Allah, shroud me all around with Your guidance. Send those around me who lead me to You and put in front of me my Lord, light and behind me, light. O' Allah, in fact make my very soul crave Your light, its guidance. And O' Allah make an abundance, an overabundance of light. Make it *'azim*. So great that the light is before me. On the Day of Judgement there will be faces that are brightened with light and others darkened with the wrath of Allah."

Allah s.w.t. described the hypocrites on the Day of Judgement in Surah al-Hadid, where when they see the believers radiant with light, they will say wait for us, let us come, so that we can share the light that the believers have been given. The believers will tell them to go back and find their own light, and a barrier will be put up between those who have genuineness of faith and the hypocrites. Light is something that radiates from the heart and that is why the Prophet said *īmān* begins in the heart, piety and the light of Allah begins in our hearts.

In Surah al-Baqarah, at the very second page when we open the e Al-Qur'an, Allah s.w.t. warns us about those whose hearts are blocked from the light of Allah. In their hearts there is sinfulness, a darkness that every time a person does something good, the angel puts a drop of light. Every time they commit a sin, a drop of darkness enters their hearts. If the darkness overwhelms the light, the heart becomes enveloped with a rusting, and that is why they do not understand the verses of Allah.

Allah s.w.t. tells us to open our hearts. "O' Allah, open my heart, open my chest, so that I can have light." Allah gives us the example of those who are spiritually dead. "I resurrected them and I gave them light. And I placed in their hearts and their chest, light." This is the *du'ā'* of the Prophet s.a.w., "O' Allah, put light in my heart. O' Allah, put light in my hearing and in my sight. O' Allah, place light above me and beneath me and to the right and to the left of me. O' Allah, put light for me in front of me and behind me. O' Allah, put within me, within my very soul, light. O' Allah, put light in abundance for me." May Allah s.w.t. lead us to His light so that we can lead others to it. May we be like as our Prophet s.a.w. who is described as a lit amber of light that surrounds.

Chapter 21

Invocation for Cure from Illnesses

اللَّهُمَّ أَذْهِبِ الْبَاسَ رَبَّ النَّاسِ، وَاشْفِ أَنْتَ الشَّافِي لَا شِفَاءَ إِلَّا شِفَاؤُكَ شِفَاءً لَا يُغَادِرُ سَقَمًا

Allahumma adhhibil-ba'sa, Rabban-nās, washfi, antash-Shāfi lā shifāa' illā shifāu'ka, shifāa'n lā yughādiru saqaman

O' Allah, do away with my suffering, O' Lord of mankind. Heal (me) as You are the only Healer and there is no cure except that of Yours, it is that which leaves no ailment behind.

(Riyad as-Salihin 902)

This is a very powerful *du'ā'*. It is a *du'ā'* that was narrated by 'Ā'ishah r.a. and she made a general but important statement in the opening of this *hadith*. This *hadith* is narrated by Imam Ibn Majah, in the chapter of medicine. This is considered as one of the medicinal formulae of the Prophet Muhammad s.a.w.; one of the Prophet s.a.w's form of spiritual treatments in treating others. 'Ā'ishah r.a. said that whenever the Prophet s.a.w. meet somebody who was complaining of pain or who was unwell, he would habitually use these particular words,

اللَّهُمَّ أَذْهِب الْبَأْسَ ، ربَّ النَّاسِ

O' my Lord, take away the pain, O' Lord of mankind

وَاشْفِ أَنْتَ الشَّافِي

Grant a cure, You are the Healer; O' Allah heal them, You are the Only Healer.

لَا شِفَاءَ إِلَّا شِفَاؤُكَ

There is no true healing, except the one You provide.

شِفَاءً لَا يُغَادِرُ سَقَمًا

Send upon them a healing that leaves no trace of this illness.

The Prophet s.a.w. would say, O' Allah, You are the Lord of mankind, remove this harm, cure them, heal them. You are the Only One who cures them and heals, O' Allah. There is no healing, no cure, no medicine, no sustenance, there is nothing that will benefit them, except that which You permitted, that which You allowed, make it a healing from You O' Allah, that leaves behind no trace of this illness. Remove and take away this pain, O' Lord of mankind. Cure them with Your curing and healing, O' Allah. Cure them as there is no cure except with You, O' Allah. It is only Your healing and no one can provide a healing except for You.

Ramadan Therapy

This means that even if a doctor provides the means towards healing or a medicine, unless You will that the medicine works O' Allah, it will not work. For some people it may work, and for some others it might not. Send upon them a healing that You have allowed to work, O' Allah. I believe that there is no healing except the one that You allowed to be healed. A healing that leaves behind no trace. It is a powerful statement of the Prophet Muhammad s.a.w. and it is worthy of reflection and analysis.

Therefore, the Prophet s.a.w. acknowledges that with sickness, ailment, pain—not only for us, but for others—this *du'ā'* is not one we just say to someone who is severely sick. It is for any illness; it is for us and for others. As a medicine, the Prophet s.a.w. would say it to those who he would visit, which teaches us an important *sunnah*. First, visiting people, especially those who are unwell. We should visit them not just in the hospital, but even if our brother is not well in his office at our workplace, pay him a visit.

If we know a neighbour who is feeling under the weather, pay them a visit. If we cannot make the distance; make a phone call, make a text, or make a *du'ā'* for them without them knowing. This *du'ā'* can be made in the presence of the person, or outside his presence. It can be made out loud that they say *āmīn* to it, or it can be made internally. It can be made for something that they are offered to drink, meaning water or something and we breathe this *du'ā'* into it and we ask them to drink it; it is also something that is accepted by the actions of the companions and the successors of Prophet s.a.w.

"Remove this pain, take away the pain O' Lord of mankind. Heal them, for You are The Healer, O' Allah. There is no healing that can come except that You have permitted, because You are The Healer, O' Allah. A healing that leaves behind no trace of this illness." Make *du'ā'* that Allah s.w.t. does not just cure us but give us back our health in a better state than what it used to be. We ask Allah s.w.t. to make this blessed month of Ramadan, a month of healing, of victory, and a month of happiness. *Allahumma āmīn.*

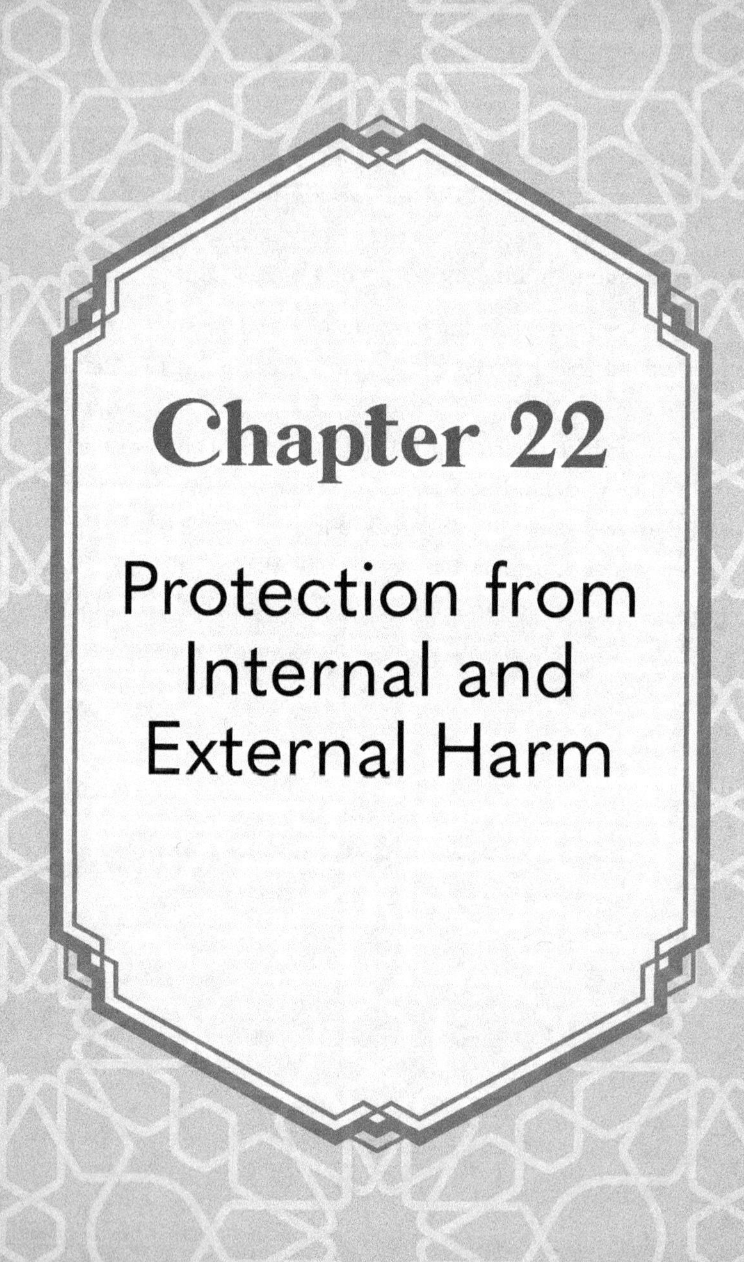

Chapter 22

Protection from Internal and External Harm

رَبِّ أَعِنِّي وَلاَ تُعِنْ عَلَيَّ وَانْصُرْنِي وَلاَ تَنْصُرْ عَلَيَّ وَامْكُرْ لِي وَلاَ تَمْكُرْ عَلَيَّ وَاهْدِنِي وَيَسِّرْ هُدَاىَ إِلَيَّ وَانْصُرْنِي عَلَى مَنْ بَغَى عَلَيَّ اللَّهُمَّ اجْعَلْنِي لَكَ شَاكِرًا لَكَ ذَاكِرًا لَكَ رَاهِبًا لَكَ مِطْوَاعًا إِلَيْكَ مُخْبِتًا أَوْ مُنِيبًا رَبِّ تَقَبَّلْ تَوْبَتِي وَاغْسِلْ حَوْبَتِي وَأَجِبْ دَعْوَتِي وَثَبِّتْ حُجَّتِي وَاهْدِ قَلْبِي وَسَدِّدْ لِسَانِي وَاسْلُلْ سَخِيمَةَ قَلْبِي

Rabbi a'inni wa la tu'in 'alayya, wansurni wa la tansur 'alayya, wamkur li, wa la tamkur 'alayya, wahdini wa yassir huda ya ilayya, wansurni 'ala mam bagha 'alayya. Allahumaj 'alni laka shaakiran, laka dhaakiran, laka raahiban, laka mitwa'an, ilaika mukhbitan, aw muniba. Rabbi taqabbal tawbati, waghsil hawbati, wa ajib da'wati, wa thabbit hujjati, wahdi qalbi wasaddid lisani, waslul sakhimata qalbi.

My Lord, help me and do not give help against me; grant me victory, and do not grant victory over me; plan on my behalf and do not plan against me; guide me, and made my right guidance easy for me; grant me victory over those who act wrongfully towards me; O' Allah, make me grateful to Thee to You, mindful of Thee to You, full of fear towards Thee to You, devoted to Thy to Your obedience, humble before Thee to You, and penitent. My Lord, accept my repentance, wash away my sin, answer my supplication, clearly establish my evidence, guide my heart, make true my tongue and draw out malice from my breast. (Sunan Abi Dawud 1510)

This *du'ā'* comes from Sunan Abi Dawud. The *hadith* is graded as Sahih by contemporary and past scholars. This is a powerful *du'ā'* of the Prophet s.a.w and it is contained under the chapter of what to say after we have said our *salam*, after we have finished our *solah*. There has always been this misconception—do we make this *du'ā'* after *solah*? The answer is yes, and there is a lot of evidence for this. There are scholars that come from the perspective or *mazhab* of Imam Ahmad and others that do not follow this tradition. In fact, it is something that is practised, and it is from the *sunnah* of the Prophet s.a.w. that we elevate our *du'ā'* in the form of *dhikr* and also in a form of petition to Allah s.w.t. when there is a need.

This *hadith* is from Abdullah ibn Abbas r.a. He said that when the Prophet s.a.w would make his *salam*, he would make this comprehensive *du'ā'*. It is recommended to say this not just after our *solah*, but anytime we feel that there is a need. The Prophet s.a.w. would say,

رَبِّ أَعِنِّي وَلاَ تُعِنْ عَلَىَّ

O' Allah, grant me Your assistance and do not help others against me. Help me, and do not let others be helped against me.

وَانْصُرْنِي وَلاَ تَنْصُرْ عَلَىَّ

Grant me victory and do not give victory to others over me.

وَامْكُرْ لِي وَلاَ تَمْكُرْ عَلَىَّ

And O' Allah, I ask You to plan for me success and do not plan for others to be successful against me.

وَاهْدِنِي وَيَسِّرْ هُدَاىَ إِلَىَّ

O' Allah, grant me guidance, and make it easy for me to be receptive and practising of that guidance.

And then the Prophet s.a.w. would say,

وَانْصُرْنِي عَلَى مَنْ بَغَى عَلَىَّ

O' Allah, grant me ascendency, conquest, and ability in victory over the ones who seek to harm me, over the ones who wronged me.

اللَّهُمَّ اجْعَلْنِي لَكَ شَاكِرًا

O' Allah, make me from those who are thankful to You, who make *shukr* to You.

لَكَ ذَاكِرًا

O' Allah, allow me to be one who makes *dhikr* of You. Remembering often of You, O' Allah.

لَكَ رَاهِبًا

O' Allah, let me be one who has turned to You, devoted, in humiliation as one who would has given his whole life towards You.

لَكَ مِطْوَاعًا

O' Allah, let me be the one who is devoted and obedient to You. That whatever You ask me to do, I will always be in Your obedience.

إِلَيْكَ مُخْبِتًا أَوْ مُنِيبًا

O' Allah, let me be from those who are humble and cast down in their humility before You.

رَبِّ تَقَبَّلْ تَوْبَتِي

O' my Lord, accept my return and repentance to You.

وَاغْسِلْ حَوْبَتِي

O' Allah, wash away my sins from me.

وَأَجِبْ دَعْوَتِي

O' Allah, answer my *du'ā'*.

وَثَبِّتْ حُجَّتِي

And O' Allah, give me clear established evidence when I need to present my case.

وَاهْدِ قَلْبِي

O' Allah, lead my heart to You, guide my heart to that which is right. Make my intentions pure.

وَسَدِّدْ لِسَانِي

O' Allah, make my tongue straightforward and true.

Ramadan Therapy

وَاسْلُلْ سَخِيمَةَ قَلْبِي

And O' Allah, draw out and remove from my heart any malice that I have towards others.

May Allah grant us the choicest of blessings by our Prophet s.a.w. This *du'ā'* is so comprehensive—"O' Allah, grant me assistance and do not assist others against me. Give me victory and salvation and do not give to others an ability to conquer me, O' Allah. Plan for my success, O' Allah, allow me to see the plan of my success, and what Your ultimate plan is for me, O' Allah. And do not make a plan for others to subdue me. And O' Allah, grant me guidance and make me willing to accept that guidance. O' Allah, give me ascendency and victory over the ones who seeks to oppress me and wrong me, O' Allah. O' Allah, let me be of those who are thankful to You, remembering of You, O' Allah. Devoted to You, obedient to You, O' Allah. O' Allah, let me be from those who have given themselves humility and penitence to You, O' Allah. O' Allah, accept my repentance. And O' Allah, wash away my sins. O' Allah, answer my *du'ā'* to You. O' Allah, give me a clear and an established evidence when I need to show my case. O' Allah, lead my heart to You and make my tongue straightforward and true. And O' Allah, let any malice be drawn out of my heart."

May Allah make this month of Ramadan a month of

rahmah, therapy, and healing for all of us. May Allah remove malice from our heart and lead our heart to truthfulness and guidance to Allah. Make us from those who have clear and established evidence and a burden of *hujjah* when it is necessary. O' Allah, answer our *du'a'* and wash away our sins. O' Allah, make us from those who are devoted to You, penitent to You, humbled to You, O' Allah. Let us be from those who are turned to You in servitude in worship and in remembrance and thankfulness, O' Allah. O' Allah give us victory against those who wronged us. O' Allah, guide us and guide our hearts to accept You and be those who follow the truth once we have heard it, O' Allah. O' Allah, make a plan for us and not a plan against us. O' Allah, give us assistance, victory, and conquest. O' Allah, assist us and do not assist others against us.

May Allah accept from us this blessed month of Ramadan. This *hadith* of Imam Abi Dawud from the words of Prophet Muhammad s.a.w. is a very important routine especially after every *solah*. May Allah make it a healing and cure as well as light and guidance for us.

Chapter 23

Supplication for Spouse, Children & Community

رَّبَّنَا هَبْ لَنَا مِنْ أَزْوَٰجِنَا وَذُرِّيَّـٰتِنَا قُرَّةَ أَعْيُنٍ وَٱجْعَلْنَا لِلْمُتَّقِيـنَ إِمَامًا (٧٤)

Rabbanā hablanā min azwā jinā wa dhurriyyātinā qurrata a'yuni waja'lnā lil muttaqīna imā ma

Our Lord, give us, from our spouses and our children, comfort of eyes, and make us heads of the God-fearing. (al-Furqan, 25:74)

The *du'ā'* that is to be shared here is a blessed *du'ā'*. It is a *du'ā'* that is from the twenty-fifth chapter of the Qur'an, Surah al-Furqan, which means The Criterion, the separation between right and wrong, or the divider. This is *āyat* number 74. Before this *āyat*, Allah s.w.t. describes and lists out the characteristics of His humble worshiping slaves, His servants. Towards the end of the *surah*, Allah s.w.t. says, that from the characteristics of the worshiping slaves of Allah, there are those who are consistent in making their invocation and *du'ā'* to Allah:

رَبَّنَا

Our Lord, *rabbana* (it is a communal *du'ā'*)

Ramadan Therapy

هَبْ لَنَا

Gift us, grace us, bless us,

مِنْ أَزْوَٰجِنَا

from our spouse—our wives in particular,

وَذُرِّيَّٰتِنَا

and from our progeny and children and offspring that come from them.

This *du'ā'* is very central for us and our family. This is a *du'ā'* of bringing about blessedness and righteousness for the future.

O' Allah, bless us with having a spouse and from our spouse; children, offspring

قُرَّةَ أَعْيُنٍ

that will be pleasing and a comfort to my eyes; *qurratun a'yun.*

Which literally means coolness to the eyes.

وَٱجْعَلْنَا لِلْمُتَّقِينَ إِمَامًا (٧٤)

And make myself and my family, all of us an imam for the believers.

158

Make us an example for the righteous to be modelled after. What a blessed *du ʿāʾ*.

At any time when Allah answers our *du ʿāʾ*, it is a gift. Therefore, understand this, that when Allah answers our *du ʿāʾ*, it is not because we have earned the right to ask for whatever we want. Whatever Allah blesses us with, we want it to be a gift from Allah, not a punishment from Allah. Sometimes Allah answers the *du ʿāʾ* of a person who is vile, gives them what they want, but in fact, it is counterproductive—even worse than if they have not received it. We do not ask for this. We ask Allah to gift us that which is good. Grant us this gift. From our spouses and children—therefore, always make in your *du ʿāʾ* the conscious effort to include ourselves, our spouse and our children.

Make it a reflective habit, that it is a reflex within us and a reflection in our mind that we will never ask only for ourselves, but also for our family. This is the righteous conduct of the Prophet s.a.w. and the Messengers and the righteous from humanity. We know Maryam's mother made a *du ʿāʾ* for her daughter when she was still in her stomach, "Make the child that is growing within me—the child, or children from him (she would assume it would be a boy) would not be touched by the *shaytān*. She made Zakariya a.s. make a *du ʿāʾ* for his unborn children. He assumed Allah would answer his *du ʿāʾ* to be gifted a son.

Ramadan Therapy

Prophet Ibrahim a.s., made a *du'ā'* for his descendants, "O' Allah make me an establisher of prayer and from my children and their progeny." He would make *du'ā'* for himself and his family—notice even in our *solah* we are commanded to say *salawat* upon Prophet Ibrahim. "O' Allah grant Your blessings and choicest of Mercy upon the Prophet Muhammad and the family of Prophet Muhammad s.a.w. *wa ala Ibrahim wa ala ali Ibrahim.*"

Therefore, have this as a statement, as a sacred formula in our *du'ā'.* From our spouse and from our offspring; *zurriyātina* literally means it comes from the concept of seed. Therefore, our children are seeds that we plant into this world that we hope will bear fruit with a tree of righteousness, *zurriyātina* that which will come from our union; that will come from our years of sacrifice, that will come from the effort we have put in their education of chasing them up and following and making sure they are habitual in their prayers.

Allah s.w.t says in Surah Ta-ha as He said to Ismail a.s and all of the Prophets of Allah, "Command your children to prayer and remain obstinately stubborn upon it." This is a recipe for success. Grant us this gift of righteousness within our spouses and our children, make them *Qurratun a'yun. Qurrata a'yun*—literally means the coolness of our eyes. The explanation of this context is, imagine we have lived in the desert of Arabia back then. There is no air conditioning, there are no goggles to protect our eyes from the desert sand, there is nothing. We would travel by camel or by horse in the desert in the scorching heat. What we would do is cover everything including our face, except for a slit of the eye so we can see where we are going, and therefore everything around us would be shielded and protected from the sun and sandblasting of the wind.

However, our eyes would bear the brunt of the elements, and that is why camels are a miraculous creation. We know they have these adaptations where their eyelashes are very particular and they are able to withstand that lashing sandblast. Once we unsaddle and come down from our horse or camel, our eyes would be burning. There would be this desert blindness that would occur, it is difficult to see and they eyes would be full of sand. Therefore, the first thing that we would get when we visit someone, or when we arrive home, was cool water that was shaded from the wind and sand, or barrels that were kept for this particular purpose.

We would basically dunk our faces in this water and open our eyes in it to clear it, and this was what was called, *qurrata a'yun*, the cleansing of the eye, the cooling of the eyes from the heat, the sand and sun, that moment of relief for our eyes that the imagery Allah says when we ask Him to make our children *qurrata a'yyun* for us, it is like we have been out in the wilderness of the world and we have come to relief by "Make my children, my spouse, the relief of my pain." What a *duʿāʾ* of therapy. A *duʿāʾ* that is necessary in Ramadan.

The second part of the *duʿāʾ*, make all of us within my family, imam of the believers; examples to model themselves after. Do not assume that it is sinful to want people to aspire to live like us. If we are modelling ourselves after the Prophet s.a.w., we are modelling ourselves after his family—his wives and children. We want to be modelled after those who lived with him, talked, and experienced the talks he gave; the life he taught and the experiences he shared with them. Therefore, we modelled ourselves with the all the imam who came before us.

O' Allah, make us imam of the believers. We want someone to look at us and our children and say, "May Allah s.w.t. bless my children to be like his children. May Allah bless me to be like him. May Allah bless my husband to be like this brother; my wife to be like this sister." May Allah s.w.t. make us the reference point of society. That people model their morality, their behaviour, their code of ethics, their conduct on us, because we modelled it from the teachings of our Prophet Muhammad s.a.w. May Allah s.w.t. also allow you to remember me and my family in our *duʿāʾ* and we pray that Allah blesses our home and family, makes our Ramadan a therapy for us and heal our grievances and connect our hearts together.

Chapter 24

Duʿāʾ that Allah Answers Immediately

لَّآ إِلَـٰهَ إِلَّآ أَنـتَ سُبْحَـٰنَكَ إِنِّى كُنتُ مِنَ الظَّـٰلِمِينَ (٨٧)

Lā ilāha illā Anta subḥānaka innī kuntu minaẓ ẓālimīn

There is no God but You. Pure are You. Indeed I was among the wrongdoers. (Surah al-Anbiya: Verse 87)

This is a *du'ā'* from the Qur'an, but there is a *hadith* that relates to it. This *du'ā'* is found in Surah al-Anbiya'. What is important about it is the pretext of it. It was reported by Saad ibn Abi Waqqas r.a., who was the uncle of the Prophet s.a.w. and one of the ten who was given the promise by the Prophet s.a.w. that he will be among of the people of Jannah. Meaning while he was still alive, the Prophet s.a.w. promised him that he would have a seat in Jannah. He was one of the greatest military generals of the *ummah*.

This hadith is found in the book of Imam at-Tirmidhi in the sunan and is from an authentic chain of narration from Saad ibn Abi Waqqas r.a as narrated to his son Muhammad, and as narrated by Muhammad to his son Ibrahim. It is also found in the Musnad of Imam Ahmad, Mustadrak of Imam al-Hakim and others. Contemporary and ancient scholars have graded them as usable and Sahih.

The Prophet s.a.w. called this the *du'ā'* of the *nun*—The Great Whale. This was the nickname of Prophet Yunus a.s. and he used this when he was ingested by the whale. Allah s.w.t. said, "Had he not been the one who is regular in making his *tasbih*? Had he not been one who is regular in his glorifications of God, He would have remained ingested by the whale until the Day of Resurrection." Allah s.w.t. reveals the *du'ā'* of the *nun* and this is one of the *du'ā'* where Allah immediately says, "*Fastajabnala,* meaning I immediately answered him."

We know the answer is immediate, because the word is not *istajabnala,* there is the *fa* that precedes it, which says *fau'taqib,* which in the Arabic language, is the *fa* of immediacy, of concurrence in immediate action. As soon as Allah received the *du'ā'* of the *nun,* it was immediately answered by Him. This is why this *du'ā'* is powerful. The Prophet s.a.w. taught it to the companions. Saad ibn Abi Waqqas said that the Prophet s.a.w. said, "The *du'ā'* he made while he was ingested in the stomach of the whale is:

لَّآ إِلَـٰهَ إِلَّآ أَنـتَ سُبْحَـٰنَكَ إِنِّـى كُنـتُ مِـنَ الظَّـٰلِمِينَ (٨٧)

Three important sentences,

لَّآ إِلَـٰهَ إِلَّآ أَنتَ

Prophet Yunus a.s. acknowledged the Supremacy of Allah. The Oneness of Allah that none is worthy of worship, but Allah. There is none that I will ever turn to and ask and seek assistance from, except You, Allah.

سُبْحَـٰنَكَ

Glorified are You, beyond perfection are You. No limitation is set upon You. No hinderance is there that is before You. No unawareness is there for You. Complete in Your Glory and unchanging in that Majesty, You will remain as You have always been.

إِنِّى

I admit.

كُنتُ مِنَ ٱلظَّـٰلِمِينَ (٨٧)

I acknowledge my sinfulness and my transgression. I am one who has wronged myself.

Three important sentences that when we put them together are a blessed *du'ā'*. The Prophet s.a.w. said, This *du'ā'* that was uttered by Prophet Yunus a.s. when he was ingested by the whale, that there is no believer who will invoke God with those same words seeking anything to have, seeking for God to fulfill something for them, in anything that they request in God, except I promise that your Lord will answer them for what they have requested, will fulfill the need that they seek, will grant them what it is that they have petitioned for, that they will be heard and answered by Allah.

Therefore, it behooves us that this *du'ā'* is important for us to make as a part of our daily rituals and part of our daily therapy in connecting with Allah s.w.t., particularly in the month of Ramadan. Three sentences—acknowledge the Maker, acknowledge the One who we worship and acknowledge the One we put our face down on the floor for and that there is nobody else that we would acknowledge in that way. Allah s.w.t. says to Prophet Musa a.s., "O' Musa, come to know that there is none worthy of worship, but Me. Only I am, I who is worthy of this." Say to them, "He is Allah the Eternal, who is Unique in His one and unity. He is the Only One of Him. There is none that can be comparable, equal to have any share with Him."

Acknowledge this as a pretext of our need.

"Glorious are You. No limit is there in You. Nothing that we can ask cannot be met. Nothing that we can seek cannot be fulfilled. There is nothing that we desire that You cannot achieve and attain for us. There is nothing that we fear that You cannot protect us from. Glorious are You in Your completeness and blessedness. Glorious are You in Your capacity to remain with Your Mercy and Compassion unchanging, even though we turn to You with sin and evil. I acknowledge, I am. It is my fault. I do not blame the *shaytān*. I do not blame the neighbours, others in my society. I acknowledge my mistake; I acknowledge my weakness. I am the one who is transgressed against my own self. I am the one who has wronged myself. I am the one who has brought myself to disrepute in harming others, taking what does not belong, looking at what is not right. Saying what is inappropriate. Doing and acting in a way that is sinful. Having financial transactions that are immoral. I acknowledge my weakness and my sinfulness before You, O' Allah."

What we will notice is that we have not made a request for what we want, but it is because Allah is the One who knows what is in our heart. Allah is the Creator and Maintainer that this is one of the most powerful *du'ā'* to get our needs fulfilled. Hence, if we are looking for marriage, for freedom, for liberty, for ease, for *rizq*, for health, for our children, for something to be blessed with or something to be removed from, for some assistance, or for removal of trial, calamity, and pestilence that has descended upon us, then this is the *du'ā'* we should make to Allah.

There is no need that we have, cut in its entirety that we make a *du'ā'* seeking Allah through this even without asking with our lips, but what is in our heart, and what Allah knows of our future will be granted for us even without specific request. May Allah make this *du'ā'* one of healing, from Surah al-Anbiya', the *du'ā'* of Prophet Yunus a.s., Jonah. May Allah make it a healing for us. *Allahumma āmīn.*

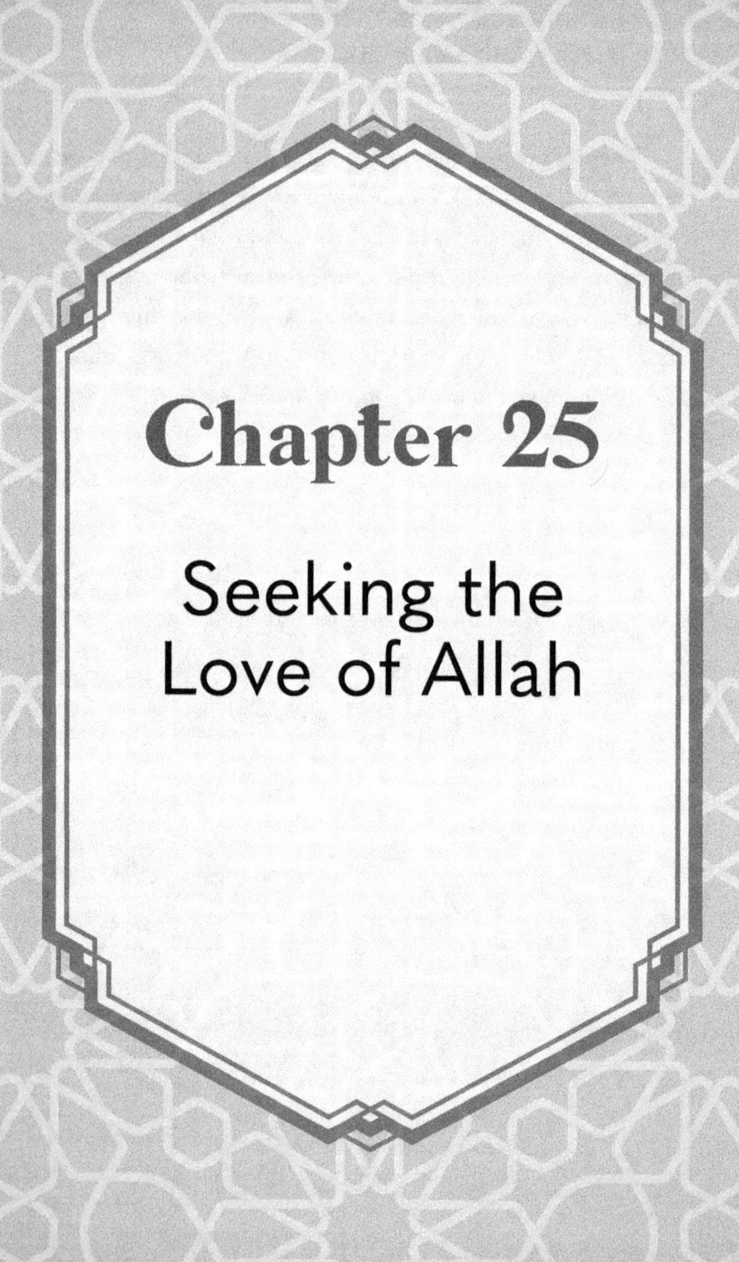

Chapter 25

Seeking the Love of Allah

اللَّهُمَّ إِنِّي أَسْأَلُكَ حُبَّكَ وَحُبَّ مَنْ يُحِبُّكَ وَالْعَمَلَ الَّذِي يُبَلِّغُنِي حُبَّكَ اللَّهُمَّ اجْعَلْ حُبَّكَ أَحَبَّ إِلَيَّ مِنْ نَفْسِي وَأَهْلِي وَمِنَ الْمَاءِ الْبَارِدِ

Allahumma innī asa'luka ḥubbaka wa ḥubba man yuḥibbuka wal-'amal al-ladhī yuballighunī ḥubbak Allahummaj'al ḥubbaka aḥabba ilaiyya min nafsī, wa ahlī wa min al-māi'l-bārid

O' Allah, indeed, I ask You for Your love and the love of those who love You, and for the action that will cause me to attain Your love, O' Allah, make Your love more beloved to me than myself, my family and cold water. (At-Tirmidhi 3490)

Ramadan Therapy

This *duʿāʾ* is of beauty, healing, and therapy. This is a *duʿāʾ* that is so significant that the Messenger s.a.w. quotes the *duʿāʾ* of a prophet. Now this is not just a *duʿāʾ* of any Prophet of God. The Prophet s.a.w. quotes this Prophet of God and he described him as this particular man who was the most serving of God, the most devoted to God, the most connected to God of those who connected themselves and were given scriptures by Allah.

This was one of the most elite amongst them, it is Prophet Dawud a.s., David. This *hadith* is also narrated by Abu Darda r.a. who was one of the *zuhad* of the *sahābah*—those who forsake the *duniya*, those who turn to the *akhirah*, those who gave a firm covenant to Allah. Those who stayed up late at night in their prayers, reciting their Qur'an and they stand before Allah. Those who were the first to give in charity and the last to take from others.

Abu Darda is from the elite of the *sahābah* and the *duʿāʾ* that he usually narrated from the Prophet s.a.w. usually run along that same vein, where he spoke about the spiritual connections of the Prophet s.a.w. This *hadith* is collected by Imam at-Tirmidhi and other scholars and graded as *hasan* and acceptable *hadith* for narration and action upon it. The Prophet s.a.w. is reported to have said, "From the *duʿāʾ* of Dawud a.s., that he used to make (and there were many of others), he would say,

اللَّهُمَّ إِنِّي أَسْأَلُكَ حُبَّكَ

O' Allah, I ask You for Your love.

وَحُبَّ مَنْ يُحِبُّكَ

And I ask You to bless to me with the love of those who love You.

وَالْعَمَلَ الَّذِي يُبَلِّغُنِي حُبَّكَ

And O' Allah, I ask You to make me love the deeds that bring me closer to Your love, that endearment, closer to You.

اللَّهُمَّ اجْعَلْ حُبَّكَ أَحَبَّ إِلَىَّ مِنْ نَفْسِي وَأَهْلِي وَمِنَ الْمَاءِ الْبَارِدِ

O' Allah, I ask You to make Your Love more dear to me, more blessed, more loved and beloved to me than what is the love that I have for myself and my family or even a sip of cold water in the heat of the day.

Allahu Akbar. What a beautiful *du'ā'* of Prophet Dawud a.s. narrated by the Prophet s.a.w. Make it a part of our repertoire that we increase our love for Allah and that Allah is beloved to us because the love of Allah is extended to us, which makes us love Him. Whenever Allah speaks to us in the Qur'an that when Allah loves us, we love Him. When He is content with us, we become content with Him. Therefore, we ask Allah for His love and that is the beginning of our relationship with God, that we ask Allah s.w.t. to love us which will make us love Allah.

Many people asked, "Shaykh, I want to increase my love for Allah, my love for the Prophet s.a.w." Know that it will only increase when the love of Allah has increased for us. We have to draw ourselves closer to Allah with the things that will endear us to Him; which will be actions that we have to perform. Therefore, pay attention now carefully towards the *du'ā*. "O' Allah, I besiege you, I beg you, I request of you, Your Love." It is not, "O' Allah, let me love You," it is "O' Allah, love me, because if You love me, I will love you. And the love of those who love You."

Why is that important? This is because those who are connected to Allah, will lead us to Allah. Those that are connected to God will invoke God on our behalf. Those who are loving Allah will increase their love and will radiate and encompass us in the love that they have for Allah. Therefore, the Prophet s.a.w. teaches us that the most sincere love is the love for another only for Allah's sake. That we should say to each other, "I love you because of my love for Allah." May Allah make us lovers of each other for the sake of Allah s.w.t.

"O' Allah I ask You, I beg You for Your Love. And the

love of those who love You. And the love of the actions that will make me love You, that will make You love me. And that I love the deeds, the actions—the *qiamullail*, the *tarawih*, the fasting in the long days, the recitation of the Qur'an even when I'm tired and bored and disconnected and cannot understand everything that I'm reciting. And the deeds that everybody resists doing, I wish to do them. O' Allah, put love in my heart for the things that are arduous to give for my wealth when I want to hoard it. To give for my health and spend it in helping and assisting others. To give for my time which is precious to me. To give from my energy and *sadaqah*, that will allow me to reach Your Love, to earn Your Love."

Therefore, the way we earn our love for Allah is through actions. It might be that these actions might be performed when we have not grown to love Allah that when we perform them, as we hope for the love of Allah; the actions that we do, will allow us to reach Your Love. "O' Allah, make Your Love more precious to me, more dear to me, more beloved by me than what I love for myself and what I would love for my family and what I would even love for a sip of cold water on a difficult and hard day."

What a powerful *du'ā'*. May Allah s.w.t. make this a *du'ā'* of healing, light, *barakah* and blessings for us. May it be a *du'ā'* that we remember on *Laylatul Qadr*. Do not forget the *du'ā'* of *Laylatul Qadr* that was in the earlier chapter.

Chapter 26

Granting Righteousness of the Soul

اللَّهُمَّ آتِ نَفْسِي تَقْوَاهَا وَزَكِّهَا أَنْتَ خَيْرُ مَنْ زَكَّاهَا أَنْتَ وَلِيُّهَا وَمَوْلَاهَا اللَّهُمَّ إِنِّي أَعُوذُ بِكَ مِنْ وَعِلْمٍ لَا يَنْفَعُ وَقَلْبٍ لَا يَخْشَعُ وَمِنْ نَفْسٍ لَا تَشْبَعُ وَدَعْوَةٍ لَا يُسْتَجَابُ لَهَا

Allahumma āti nafsī taqwāhā, wa zakkihā anta khairu man zakkāhā, anta waliyyuhā wa mawlāhā. Allahumma innī a'udhū bika min 'ilmin lā yanfa'u wa qalbin la yakhsha'u wa min nafsin lā tashba'u wa da'watin lā yustajābu lahā

O' Allah, make my soul obedient and purify it, for You are The Best One to purify it, You are its Guardian and Lord. O' Allah, I seek refuge in You from a heart that is not humble, a soul that is not satisfied, knowledge that is of no benefit and a supplication that is not answered.
(Sunan an-Nasa'i 5458)

Ramadan Therapy

This is a *du'a'* that is dear to the heart. It is a *du'a'* of the Prophet s.a.w. where he gathered some of the great issues that we all deal with in our life. It is a *du'a'* that adjusts our inconsistencies and rebalances our approaches in dealing with Allah s.w.t. and in the expression of Islam that we show to each other in society. We ask Allah sw.t. in this blessed month of Ramadan, to grant us an inner awakening of *taqwa* that is within our privacy and private life and greater in merit and reward than what we seek to show each other and in our public portrayal.

This is a *du'a'* that is collected by Imam Muslim. The Prophet s.a.w. would say,

$$\text{اللَّهُمَّ آتِ نَفْسِي تَقْوَاهَا}$$

"O' Allah, grant my soul a sense of righteousness." This is powerful. Make our piety inward. Make our piety for the soul, not just of outward bodily function alone. This is in tune with the *hadith* of Prophet s.a.w., also in Sahih Muslim, where he would point to his heart as report by Abu Hurairah r.a. and he would say, "*Taqwa* is inside here." (Sahih Muslim 2564a) It is in our soul. It is part of who we are and the ideals that we have. The Prophet s.a.w. would say,

$$\text{وَزَكِّهَا أَنْتَ خَيْرُ مَنْ زَكَّاهَا}$$

"And O' Allah, purify my *taqwa*, purify my righteousness, You are the best of purifiers." Now, this is important, it is not just that we want *taqwa*, but O' Allah, we want the best of *taqwa*. When we talk about men in our places for example, we have this concept of chivalry. In chivalry we do not choose what is right from what is wrong, but we choose what is most right from what is right. It is a different way of looking at this. Here we have evidence of the Prophet s.a.w. asking and invoking Allah to purify his soul as Allah s.w.t. commands us in the Qur'an, where we ask Allah to give us *taqwa* of our soul. This is the *du'ā'* of the Prophet s.a.w., You are the best of purifiers.

أَنْتَ وَلِيُّهَا وَمَوْلَاهَا

"O' Allah, You are the Protecting Friend of my soul and the Guardian of it. You are my Protector, and the Guardian of my soul." This shows us that Allah s.w.t. can become two very important aspects of our life. He can become One who protects our soul from sinfulness and the desires that we do not seek to fulfill in an evil sinful manner. This is also to guard us from seeking harm from other people and other things. Protecting us from harm and guarding us against fulfilling harm and oppression towards other people.

Once again, the Prophet s.a.w. would say, "O' Allah, grant my soul its *taqwa*, righteousness. Its consciousness of You. And purify my soul, O' Allah, for You are the best to purify and to make my soul one in a sanctified state. You are its Protector, You are the One who protects me from wronging myself, from wronging others from that which would encroach upon me; from the evil presence of the *shaytān*, from the whisperings of the devil and from the envy of others and You are its Governor. You are the One who can restrain me and restrain it from that which is a sinful impulse that I ask You to protect me from."

اللَّهُمَّ إِنِّي أَعُوذُ بِكَ مِنْ عِلْمٍ لاَ يَنْفَعُ

Then the Prophet would continue and say, "O' Allah, I besiege you to protect me from knowledge that is of no benefit to me." And that is really important. Therefore, after he asked for *taqwa*, he speaks about knowledge. Knowledge is the thing that leads us to *taqwa*. It is a thing that leads us to understanding the cognisance of God—understanding our place with Allah s.w.t. The Prophet s.a.w. says, "O' Allah, make my *taqwa* towards You alone. Purify it, O' Allah."

Second, the Prophet s.a.w. says, "O' Allah, bless me with knowledge that is beneficial." This means knowledge that is actionable that we put in our service, that we use in that which is pleasing to You, O' Allah. Therefore, there are two levels of knowledge. There is knowledge that is discussed in the Qur'an. That there are people who were given knowledge, but it led them further away from God. We ask Allah s.w.t. to protect us from this.

This *du'ā'* where Prophet s.a.w. said, "O' Allah, I ask You to bless me, to protect me with the blessing of protection from knowledge that does not benefit." Therefore, there are two ways how the Prophet s.a.w. would invoke Allah for knowledge. "O' Allah, give us beneficial knowledge" and he would also say, "O' Allah protect us from knowledge that is not beneficial" which is a powerful way of establishing the importance of this very central process. We ask Allah to bless us with good knowledge that we use and to protect us from knowledge that leads us away from Him that is sinful in its discourse and intention.

اللَّهُمَّ إِنِّي أَعُوذُ بِكَ مِنْ قَلْبٍ لاَ يَخْشَعُ

O' Allah, protect us from a heart that cannot humble to You.

وَمِنْ نَفْسٍ لاَ تَشْبَعُ

And from a soul that continues to crave and has no contentment and has no limit in its cravings, in its desire for more.

وَدَعْوَةٍ لاَ يُسْتَجَابُ لَهَا

And from a *du'ā'* that I make to You, O' Allah that is not heard and that is not answered by You.

Ramadan Therapy

SubhanAllah. Look at this beautiful *du'ā'*. "O' Allah, protect me from knowledge that is not of benefit to me and others. O' Allah, protect me from a heart that does not humble itself to Allah." Allah s.w.t. says is it not time for the believers that they should come to an awareness of the heart that it should humble itself to the orders of Allah and what has been revealed for its truth. We ask Allah s.w.t. to give us the heart of a sparrow, a heart that is soft, that is malleable—not a heart that is rock solid. In fact, there are hearts that are harder than rocks.

May Allah protect us from a heart that cannot humble itself to Allah. *Khusyuk* is one thing that is silent, quiet and refers to a heart that is still when it needs to be still. May Allah protect us and give this. To protect us from a soul that cannot find contentment, that cannot come to a point and say, "I have had enough", at times a soul craves so much. At times that it fears poverty, but at times, it is poverty that has the remedy and the medicine for many of us. May Allah give us the medicine that we need, that will give us a place with Him in Jannah.

O' Allah, make our souls content, protect us from a soul that cannot be content. O' Allah, protect us from a *du'ā'* that is not heard. Yes, my brothers and sisters, there are moments where we make *du'ā'* and we are unworthy of being heard by Allah. In a *hadith* of Imam Muslim, the Prophet s.a.w tells of the man who is lost in the desert, he has no hope of survival, so he puts his hands to the sky and said, "My Lord, my Lord (in asking for help)." (Sahih Muslim 1015). However, his food is from the haram, his clothing is from the haram, his whole life is sustained in haram, how does he expect to be answered by Allah, who is The One who answers, especially for those who are in need. We ask Allah to not turn us away from Him without being answered, without being heard. O' Allah, protect us from a *du'ā'* that is not answered.

O' Allah, grant our soul its *taqwa*. Bless it O 'Allah, bless us with purification, meaning to make *tazkiyah*—to cleanse what is wrong and to put in its place, and *tarbiyah*, establish what is right. You are its Protector and Guardian. O' Allah, I ask You to protect us from knowledge that is of no benefit, from a heart and soul that cannot find contentment, from a heart that cannot find humility and from a *du'ā'* that is not answered. May Allah protect us from all of that.

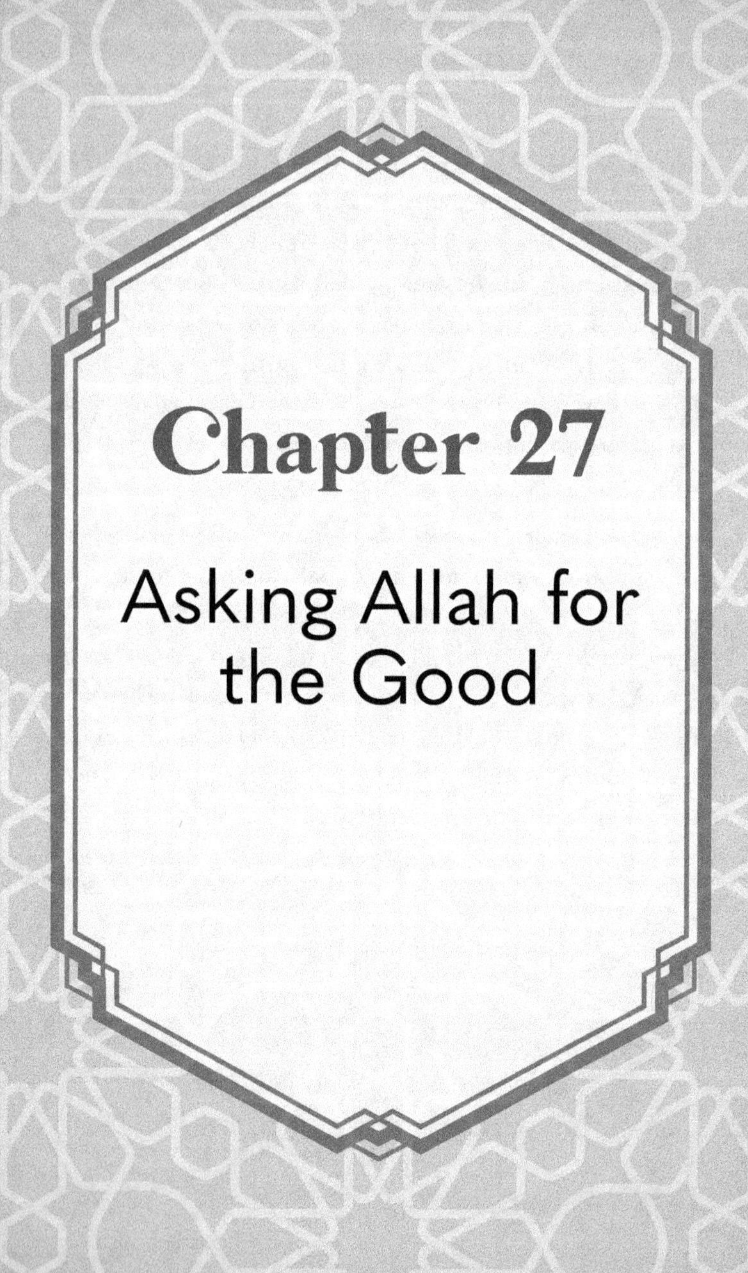

Chapter 27

Asking Allah for the Good

اللَّهُمَّ إِنِّي أَسْأَلُكَ مِنَ الْخَيْرِ كُلِّهِ عَاجِلِهِ وَآجِلِهِ
مَا عَلِمْتُ مِنْهُ وَمَا لَمْ أَعْلَمْ وَأَعُوذُ بِكَ مِنَ الشَّرِّ
كُلِّهِ عَاجِلِهِ وَآجِلِهِ مَا عَلِمْتُ مِنْهُ وَمَا لَمْ أَعْلَمْ
اللَّهُمَّ إِنِّي أَسْأَلُكَ مِنْ خَيْرِ مَا سَأَلَكَ عَبْدُكَ
وَنَبِيُّكَ وَأَعُوذُ بِكَ مِنْ شَرِّ مَا عَاذَ بِهِ عَبْدُكَ
وَنَبِيُّكَ اللَّهُمَّ إِنِّي أَسْأَلُكَ الْجَنَّةَ وَمَا قَرَّبَ إِلَيْهَا
مِنْ قَوْلٍ أَوْ عَمَلٍ وَأَعُوذُ بِكَ مِنَ النَّارِ وَمَا
قَرَّبَ إِلَيْهَا مِنْ قَوْلٍ أَوْ عَمَلٍ وَأَسْأَلُكَ أَنْ تَجْعَلَ
كُلَّ قَضَاءٍ قَضَيْتَهُ لِي خَيْرًا

Allahumma inni as'aluka minal-khayri kullihi, 'ajilihi wa ajilihi, ma 'alimtu minhu wa ma la a'lam. Wa a'udhu bika minash-sharri kullihi, 'ajilihi wa ajilihi, ma 'alimtu minhu wa ma la a'lam. Allahumma inni as'aluka min khayri ma sa'alaka 'abduka wa nabiyyuka, wa a'udhu bika min sharri ma 'adha bihi 'abduka wa nabiyyuka. Allahumma inni as'alukal-jannata wa ma qarraba ilayha min qawlin aw 'amalin, wa a'udhu bika minan-nari wa ma qarraba ilayha min qawlin aw 'amalin, wa as'aluka an taj'al kulla qada'in qadaytahuli khayran

Ramadan Therapy

O' Allah, I ask You for all that is good, in this world and in the Hereafter, what I know and what I do not know. O' Allah, I seek refuge with You from all evil, in this world and in the Hereafter, what I know and what I do not know. O' Allah, I ask You for the good that Your slave and Prophet has asked You for, and I seek refuge with You from the evil from which Your slave and Prophet sought refuge. O' Allah, I ask You for Paradise and for that which brings one closer to it, in word and deed, and I seek refuge in You from Hell and from that which brings one closer to it, in word and deed. And I ask You to make every decree that You decree concerning me, good. (Sunan Ibn Majah 3846)

This is a *du'ā'* from the *sunnah*, collected by Imam Ibn Majah. It is from the statement of 'Ā'ishah r.a and the *hadith* is guarded as Sahih. 'Ā'ishah r.a. said, "The Prophet s.a.w. dictated and taught me this particular *du'ā*.'" Now there are other narrations of this *du'ā'* with slightly different wordings from other *sahābah*.

A person came to the Messenger of Allah and asked, "O' Prophet s.a.w., I wish to invoke God of things you invoke, but I do not know everything that you have asked for. I do not know what good to ask for, and what bad to ask Allah to protect me from." The Prophet s.a.w. then taught him this *du'ā'* as he had also taught to his wife. This shows us that this *du'ā'* is like a prescribed medicine by the Prophet Muhammad s.a.w. We ask Allah to make this Ramadan a month of healing, therapy, and reunion with those we have been cut off in the distance. The *du'ā'* begins with the Prophet s.a.w. acknowledging the Creator Allah s.w.t. We begin by saying:

اللَّهُمَّ إِنِّي أَسْأَلُكَ مِنَ الْخَيْرِ كُلِّهِ عَاجِلِهِ وَآجِلِهِ مَا عَلِمْتُ مِنْهُ وَمَا لَمْ أَعْلَمْ

The first sentence of the *du'ā'* is, "O' Allah, I ask You for all the good, all of it, the good, O' Allah that is in this world and that which is said in store for the next life. That is near to me, that I can acquire it in this life, and after my time on this Earth has come to an end (death), let there be *khayr* for me, what I know of and what I do not know of." *SubhanAllah,* what a profound statement and *du'ā'* of the Prophet s.a.w.

There are some things that are *khayr* for us that we cannot immediately see. We do not see that there is good in that illness. We do not see that there is good perhaps in that divorce, we do not see that there is good for not being accepted into that school or attaining that job or promotion. Therefore, the Prophet s.a.w. said, "O' Allah, open my heart, open my eyes to see the good, what I can recognise and understand, what I can perceive and what I do not."

وَأَعُوذُ بِكَ مِنَ الشَّرِّ كُلِّهِ عَاجِلِهِ وَآجِلِهِ مَا عَلِمْتُ مِنْهُ وَمَا لَمْ أَعْلَمْ

The other side of asking Allah for what is good, we also ask Allah to protect us from evil. The Prophet s.a.w. then said, "O' Allah, I ask for protection in You." When we say, "I seek refuge with you O' Allah, I ask for protection…" —it acknowledges three things. One, that Allah is the Only One to protect. He is the Only One who can assist us from harm once it has befallen and to protect us before it arrives. Next, we know that there is danger in the world and that we live our life with an acute sense of *taqwa*; awareness from dealings with Allah s.w.t.

"O' Allah protect me from evil. The evil that I create within my life, that I bring upon through my sinfulness and my indiscretions. And the evil of others, the envy, the anger, the hatred, the wrath, the jealousy that others may have of me. From all types of evil; all of evil—whether it is residing in this life, something that I can experience in this life, or that which is set in store for the next life. O' Allah, change our ways so that we do not find wretchedness and hardship in the next life. From that which we have recognised the danger and the evil and that which I am oblivious of." May Allah protect us from being blindsided by sinfulness and evil at entering our life. Then the Prophet s.a.w. said,

اللَّهُمَّ إِنِّي أَسْأَلُكَ مِنْ خَيْرِ مَا سَأَلَكَ عَبْدُكَ وَنَبِيُّكَ

O' Allah, I ask You from the best of things that were asked of You by Your Prophet and Your Messenger, Muhammad s.a.w.

وَأَعُوذُ بِكَ مِنْ شَرِّ مَا عَاذَ بِهِ عَبْدُكَ وَنَبِيُّكَ

And I ask You, O' Allah, to protect me from the things that Your Prophet and Your Messenger asked You to protect him from. O' Allah, give us what the Prophet asked for and protect us from what the Prophet asked to be protected from. *Allahumma āmīn*

The next part of the *du'ā'*,

اللَّهُمَّ إِنِّي أَسْأَلُكَ الْجَنَّةَ

O' Allah, I ask you for Jannah.

وَمَا قَرَّبَ إِلَيْهَا مِنْ قَوْلٍ أَوْ عَمَلٍ

And whatever means of words or actions that will draw me closer to it.

"O' Allah, I ask you for Jannah, but I recognise that I must invest myself in this life. Therefore O' Allah, give me the words and the actions I need to perform to bring me closer to You." O' Allah, bring us closer to Jannah with our words and deeds.

وَأَعُوذُ بِكَ مِنَ النَّارِ

And O' Allah, I ask You to protect me from hellfire. Protect us from the Hellfire. Protect us from its blaze and its torment, O' Allah.

وَمَا قَرَّبَ إِلَيْهَا مِنْ قَوْلٍ أَوْ عَمَلٍ

O' Allah, protect us from what brings us close to the Hellfire with words or deeds. May Allah protect us from those words and deeds that bring Hellfire closer to us and bring us closer to it. *Allahumma āmīn.* Look at the symmetry of the *du'ā'*, there is both for Jannah and Hellfire.

وَأَسْأَلُكَ أَنْ تَجْعَلَ كُلَّ قَضَاءٍ قَضَيْتَهُ لِي خَيْرًا

And the final part of the *du'ā'*. "O' Allah, I ask You, I beg of You to make every *qada'*, every decision, every ordainment, every fated decision You have made for me and my future life, that You make it good for me. *Allahumma āmīn"*

O' Allah, that marriage that one may be seeking. O' Allah, that job that we are applying for. O' Allah, that position at school that we wish to attain as a student. O' Allah, that entrance exam that we are about to write. O' Allah, this driving test we are going to make. O' Allah, this investment we are going to do. O' Allah, whatever *qada'* that is to come in my future that is yet to be to formulated, that has not yet come to past, make it *khayr* for me. May Allah s.w.t. make our *qada'*, make His decree for us, concerning us and our families always good. We ask Allah s.w.t. to give us the best of *qada'* in this blessed last 10 nights of Ramadan. We ask Allah to bless us with happiness and contentment in this life and the next. May this Ramadan be a month of happiness and therapy.

Chapter 28

Duʿāʾ of
Guidance, Piety,
Chastity and
Affluence

اللَّهُمَّ إِنِّي أَسْأَلُكَ الْهُدَى وَالتُّقَى وَالْعَفَافَ وَالْغِنَى

Allahumma inni as aluka al huda wattuqa wal 'afaf wal ghina

O' Allah. I beg of Thee the right guidance, safeguard against evils, chastity and freedom from want. (Sahih Muslim 2721a)

This *du'ā'* is comprised of four important words. A *du'ā'* of just four words? Yes! It is a *du'ā'* that was habitually made by the Prophet s.a.w. and heard by the *sahābah*. It is something that he would say in his *solah*, there are narrations of it. After the *solah*, it would be something that he would say when he was moving about. It would be something that he would say when he was seated or reclining in the company of others. It is one of those multipurpose invocations, and we will understand why.

The Prophet s.a.w. would ask for four things. Four particular words. He asked for guidance, he asked for righteousness and piety, he asked for chastity and he asked for affluence. Each of those are four things we esteem and want in life. They are the basis of all the relationships that we have in life.

What is this *du'ā'* of the Prophet s.a.w.?

اللَّهُمَّ

"O' Allah, my Lord, You are the Only One I turn to in worship." That is the word of *Allahumma*. To You alone Allah, I make this request, this petition, this invocation and the supplication of seeking.

اللَّهُمَّ إِنِّي أَسْأَلُكَ الْهُدَى

"I ask of this; I request of You. O' Allah, I beg You, I ask You, I supplicate, I invoke You to bless me with *al-Huda*. Guidance." There are two levels of guidance. There is guidance of seeing—*basīrah*, where we see guidance, so it inspires us. We read a book, we read a *hadith* or had a discussion with others that moved our heart to action. This is a guidance of Allah showing us the way in a practical and real sense.

There is also a second guidance, which is an esoteric, internal guidance. That which is the guidance of our heart being moved by Allah. We know that Allah s.w.t. is the Governor of the hearts. Allah alternates the heart as He sees fit. As Allah s.w.t. determines in His decree. When we are asking for *hidayah*, make sure in our intention, that we are asking for both. "O' Allah, let somebody lead me to something which is good. Let me find the truth. O' Allah, let me hear of it, read of it, witness it, let me be a person who recognises the *āyat* that You have sent." Allah says, "I will show them the signs". Therefore, "O' Allah, open my eyes to these signs."

In addition, make our intention based on the *hidayah* that we are asking for. The *huda* that we are asking for, is that our heart opens. That was what Prophet Musa a.s. asked for. That was what the Prophet was given, through Surah al-Insyirah. This is the second level of *hidayah*. It is inspired by Allah where Allah casts into the heart a sense of softness that opens it to accept the truth and that it sees the truth with its eyes and hears the truth with its ears. May Allah give us both levels of the guidance. Sadly, many will see guidance with their eyes, but their hearts would not recognise it. Allah warns of this in the Qur'an—it is not that the eyes are blind and they cannot see the reality, but it is that the chest contains a heart that has no perception and is dimmed to the truth. (al-Hajj, 22:46). "O' Allah I ask You for the two levels of guidance."

وَالتُّقَى

And O' Allah, bless me with *taqwa*. O' Allah, bless me with guidance and piety. Piety is the thing we need to discover through guidance and Allah tells us this in the beginning of Surah al-Baqarah, "This book is a guidance to those who possess piety." Therefore, to receive that piety, to ask Allah to open our heart, to show us the truth so that we can follow it and practise it, requires a sincerity of heart, a piety of purpose and being in a soul. Piety is internal, it is not just a feeling in the heart. *Īmān* which is in the heart, it is not what one hopes for. It is what takes residence in the heart and is proven through deeds—the actions that you perform.

Therefore *īmān*, the purpose of *īmān* and *taqwa*, which are interchangeable, *at-tuqqa* means faith in Allah, that faith is in our heart, but it must be proven through deeds. The Prophet s.a.w. was asking, "O' Allah, show me guidance which is what I will believe in my heart and give me *taqwa* which is the actions of my body." Whenever *taqwa* is referred to in the Qur'an and the tradition, it means deeds, not just belief in the heart.

وَالْعَفَافَ

O' Allah, grant us chastity. May Allah grant us, our family, our homes, our children and offspring, chastity. A sense of '*Iffa*. '*Iffatunnafs*, that there is a chastity of the soul, where we do not seek what people have. We are not jealous, we are not greedy, we are someone who is content with what Allah has given, we aspire to greatness, but if we do not achieve it because it is sinful to be achieved in the way that others have, then we are happy to be where we are because that is better for us in our *duniya* and *akhirah*. '*Iffatunnafs* is that we do not seek excessiveness, we have an ability to feel *qanaah*—that we have enough, and Allah has blessed us with much and we are thankful for it. To be a person of *afaf*, is that we are able to control our bodily organs. In particular, the three most important—eyes, the tongue and the private part. That we are able to control our sexual desires. We are able to control our verbal impulses and we are able to cast away our eyes from that which is sinful. We ask Allah s.w.t. for guidance, piety and chastity.

And O' Allah, enrich us. The Prophet s.a.w. said, *ghina, ghinannafs*. True affluence is that our soul can find contentment. It is internal ,and therefore to be affluent is a blessed thing, that Allah gives us from the different kind of worldly material is a blessed thing. We should all aspire to be multimillionaires, not just millionaires. May Allah bless us all with a vastness of *rizq*, that we earn from the halal. These are the two conditions. Earn in halal and spend it on halal and give of its share in *zakah* as it is due.

May Allah s.w.t. give us affluence, but recognise that the greatest affluence is the enrichment of the soul. That a person is able to be content. Therefore, we see, *al-afaf* and *ghina*. O' Allah, give us chastity, and O' Allah, enrich us. *Allahumma āmīn*. May Allah give us this affluent enrichment, where we recognise and praise Allah. Do not ever feel shy about craving our share for the *duniya*, working hard, saving well and being economically empowered. Those are all things that are from the *sunnah* of the Prophet and the *sahābah*.

The hand that gives is better than the hand that receives. The one who shares is better than the one who is shared with. The one who is strong in mind, in heart, in *īmān*, in economic prosperity, is more beloved to Allah that the one who is poor and weak. All of these are from the tradition and the authentic words of the Prophet s.a.w. So we make this *du'ā'* to Allah. Four words. O' Allah, bless us, give us guidance, piety, chastity, and affluence. *Allahumma āmīn*.

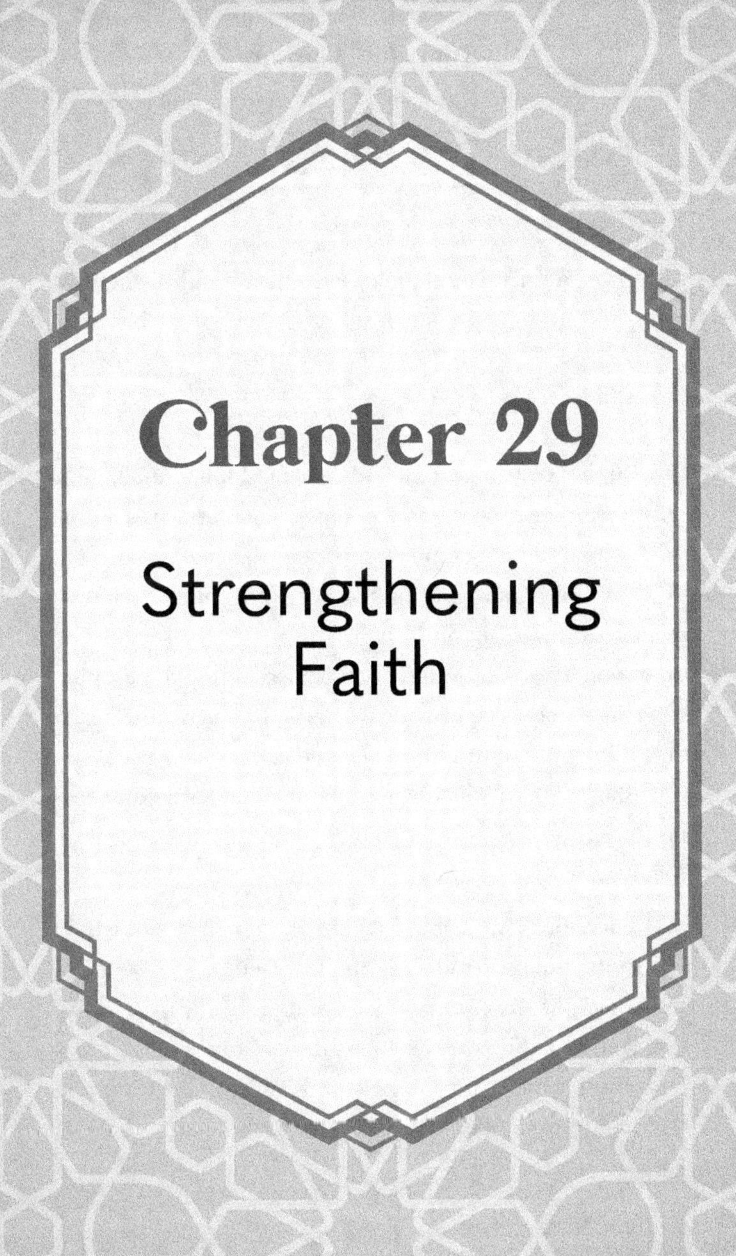

Chapter 29

Strengthening Faith

اللَّهُمَّ ثَبِّتْ قَلْبِي عَلَى دِينِكَ

Allahumma thabbit qalbī ʿalā dīnika

O' Allah, make my heart steadfast in (adhering to) Your religion (Sunan Ibn Majah 3834)

This is a very important and dear *du ʿā'*. It is a small, short *du ʿā'* that we hope to continue in practice. It is a *du ʿā'* that is reported of Prophet s.a.w. and the *du ʿā'* is narrated by Anas ibn Malik r.a. In the previous chapters, it was mentioned that Anas ibn Malik was one of the servants of the Prophet s.a.w. His mother dedicated him to the Prophet s.a.w. as a young child and she said, "I want you to teach the child and I want him to accompany you. He will carry your shoes. He will fetch you water and whatever you need. Just have him near you in your presence, O' Messenger of Allah, s.a.w."

Therefore, Anas ibn Malik grew up in a household and in the times surrounding the Prophet s.a.w. as a young child and into his young teen years. The Prophet s.a.w. would educate him every step of the way. One of the things we noticed about Anas ibn Malik is that the *du ʿā'* that he reported from the Prophet s.a.w. are very similar to the *du ʿā'* that the Prophet's wives report from him. This *du'ā'* was reported by Ummu Salamah r.a. and others.

It is a *du'ā'* that is famous from the Prophet s.a.w. where he invokes Allah s.w.t. to grant stability to faith in his heart. Now ponder on that for a second. The Messenger of Allah, the one who receives revelation, the one who is exposed to the angels, the one who Jibril strengthens, and is his guardian angel. That Messenger of Allah, that Prophet of Allah s.a.w. asked Allah to keep his heart firm upon conviction of faith? The answer is yes. There is a beautiful *hadith* which is found in the books of Imam Ibn Majah and others, it is an authentic *hadith* of the Prophet s.a.w. Anas ibn Malik said, the Prophet s.a.w. was often heard saying,

اللَّهُمَّ ثَبِّتْ قَلْبِي عَلَى دِينِكَ

"O 'Allah, keep my heart firm, keep my heart steadfast in adherence to this *deen*, to this way of life, this faith, this religion." A man asked, "O' Messenger of Allah, do you fear for us even though we have already come to believe in you and we have accepted what you have brought for us from Allah?" Therefore, we see the subtlety of this *du'ā'*. The Prophet s.a.w. when he taught the *sahābah du'ā'*, he would not say, "You say, because you lack faith." He would make it something as a part of his *du'ā'*, his repertoire, his regular practice. When the Prophet s.a.w. would practise, he said,

"I make *taubat* to Allah and *istighfar* to Allah more than a hundred times a day." It is not because he is sinning more than a hundred times a day, but he wants us to be inspired by that action. He takes it upon himself to model that behavior.

In the Qur'an, in Surah at-Tawbah verse 128, Allah s.w.t says, "I have sent you a Messenger from your own kind", which Prophet Muhammad s.a.w. said, "Hold on strictly to my tradition and practice and the tradition of those who will follow me in that behaviour from the *khulafa'*, those who will be with you after me, his *sahābah* in their entirety; not one or two individuals, but their collection as a community." Allah s.w.t. says, "*Uswatun hasanah*; that I have sent you Muhammad s.a.w. as the greatest model of example for you to practise."

The *sahābah* understood that the Prophet s.a.w. does not have weakness of faith and that his heart would never stray away from Allah and he does not need to ask Allah s.w.t. so repetitively of this *duʿā'*. In one *Riwāyat*, it goes, "O' Allah, who keeps the heart steadfast, make my heart steadfast." Here the Prophet s.a.w. said, "O' Allah, make my heart firm, steadfast upon this path of truth, this way of life, this submission to you, this *deen* that you have sent." The path that is accepted by God as a way of life, is submission to Him.

The *sahābah* also understood that the Prophet s.a.w. is making this *duʿā'* to influence them in their thoughts, in their behaviour that they take it as a counsel within themselves, "My heart is something that I should check, my heart is something that I should feel." The man then asked the Messenger of Allah, "Do you fear for us after we believe in you and accepted what you have brought to us, that we would revert back?" The Prophet s.a.w. said, "The hearts of the individual are between the fingers of Allah s.w.t., He turns them as He wishes."

That statement, we leave it as it was mentioned by the Prophet s.a.w. The two fingers of Allah, we do not change its meaning, convolute it or alter it, we state it as what was stated by the Prophet s.a.w., but equally as important, we do not let our minds give conjecture to it and say well, this is a similitude and anthropomorphism, it is a likeness to humanity. Part of our *aqidah* as Muslims, is that there is nothing in existence like the Existence of Allah. Even though the names are associated to the things that we understand, Allah is Majestically Elevated above any likeness that we can have. Therefore, when Allah s.w.t. refers to His Hands of giving, His Hands of Mercy, The Eyes that He witnesses us with, they are not to be made subjected to what we understand in reality.

Thus, the Hand of Allah s.w.t. is not like our hand.

Ramadan Therapy

It is not like the hands of time, which are proverbial, it is not like the hands of our created beings, it is unique to the uniqueness of Allah s.w.t., We leave the word as Allah has said it and we do not assign to it a particular meaning that will change it from its essence as mentioned by Allah s.w.t. and we push away any thought of anthropomorphism, or any modelling of Allah s.w.t.

However, Allah s.w.t. as described by the Prophet s.a.w., is that our hearts are controlled by Him. They are within His grasp, within His turn, that He turns our hearts towards and away from Him. We ask Allah to keep our hearts with Allah s.w.t. O' Allah, keep our hearts firm upon this faith, keep our hearts firm upon *īmān*, keep our hearts firm upon this *tawhid* of singling You out in all aspects of worship. *Allahumma āmīn.*

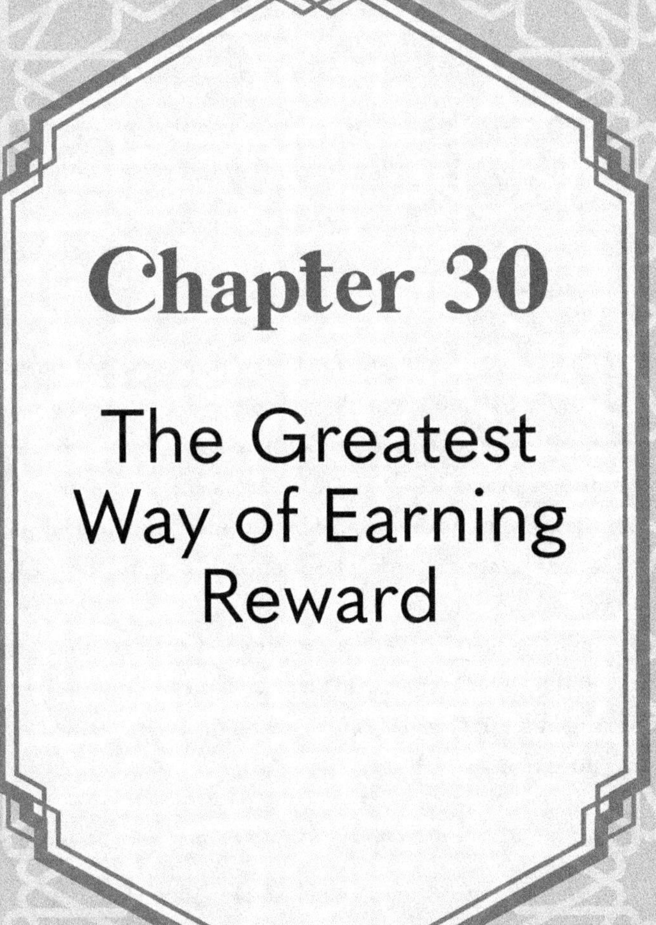
Chapter 30

The Greatest
Way of Earning
Reward

سُبْحَانَ اللَّهِ وَبِحَمْدِهِ، سُبْحَانَ اللَّهِ الْعَظِيم

SubhanAllahi wa bihamdihi; SubhanAllahil 'Azim,

Allah is free from imperfection and all praise is due to Him; Allah is free from imperfection, The Greatest (Sahih Bukhari 6682)

———◆———

This *du'ā'* is the very final recorded *hadith* by Imam Bukhari in his Sahih collection of *hadith*. This is narrated by Abu Hurairah r.a. It is a *hadith* that we are familiar with and let us ensure we know this *dhikr* and *du'ā'*. It is powerful and one that fills the scale on the Day of Judgement with reward. The Prophet s.a.w. was heard to have said, and this is narrated by many of the books and chains of collection, "There are two statements that are beloved by The Merciful, Allah s.w.t. Nevertheless, they are very light on the tongue, but heavy on the scales of the Day of Judgement."

سُبْحَانَ اللهِ وَبِحَمْدِهِ، سُبْحَانَ اللهِ الْعَظِيم

Two statements that are beloved by Allah, The Lord of Mercy. One of the *du'ā'* we studied is that we ask Allah s.w.t., "O' Allah, we ask You for Your Love and the love of those who love You and the love of the deeds that earn Your love." This is one of those deeds. These two statements are beloved by Allah. Each of them individually is loved by Allah, not just as a collection for both of them, but when we put them together, they are even more blessed and loved by Allah.

Therefore, on their own, *SubhanAllah wa bihamdih*, on its own, is a blessing. It has many different *hadith* and *du'a'* as mentioned by the Prophet s.a.w. It is something we say in our sujud, *Subhanallahi wa bihamdih*. Prophet s.a.w. said in an authentic *hadith* in Bukhari and Muslim that the one who says this a hundred times in their day, their sins are forgiven even if they were to envelope and cover the oceans. The other one is *Subhanallahil 'azim*, which is what we say in our *ruku'*. This is a natural habit of a believer. To be excessive, consistent, praising of Allah s.w.t. with these two particular *du'a'*.

Why are they so significant? Both of them begin with, *subhan*. The word *subhan*, *Subhan Allah*, it comes from *sa-ba-ha*, which means an infinite process. Something of which we do not know its limit. We cannot estimate where it ends or where it begins. Therefore Allah s.w.t., when we say, limitless is Your Glory, O' Allah—nothing could ever take away from Your Completeness, O' Allah. There is no change to Your Grandeur, Your Majesty and Your Magnificence, O' Allah. There is nothing that alters Your *Rahmah*, O' Allah. There is nothing that changes Your greatest qualities, O' Allah.

Subhan Allah and therefore, we say this as an exclamation towards something beautiful or also something repugnant.

When we hear the claims of those who claim that Allah has offspring, a child, a son, a shared accomplice in this world, say, *SubhanAllah*. How could someone say this? They claimed that the Majestic, *ar-Rahman* the Lord of Mercy, has begotten a child. *Subhana*, glorified in His limitlessness He is beyond this need. And All Praises are due to Him. The *Hamd* of Allah, applies to two things—it means that we elevate Allah, and we limit it from anyone other than Him. Therefore, we make this *Hamd* and praise Allah in a way that nobody else can be deserving of it. In a way that nobody else is worshipped.

That is the secret of us making this in our sujud, because we will never make *sujud* to anyone but Allah. He is the Only One worthy of our servitude and enslavement. We end by claiming, we are attesting, our statement, our conviction, our belief, that Allah is *al-'Azim*. He is Greater than all things. He is Mightier than all things. Whatever problems that we have, dear brother and sister, Allah is there. Whatever hardship we face, Allah is there. The *du'a'* above is light upon the tongue, but heavy on the scales of the Day of Judgment.

Imam Bukhari on the last chapter of his collection is about *tawhid*; the uniqueness of Allah in our worship of Allah as being the Only One that is Eternal, in His uniqueness s.w.t. Imam Bukhari narrated this *hadith*, one, because the most perfect of way to end a book of *hadith* with the greatest ways of earning reward for it is to ask Allah through these words. In addition, it also shows us the conviction that we have that we will be questioned about how we have lived. Our deeds will be weighed, and if we know that we are light in good deeds due to other reasons, then fill it up. Fill it up with simple statements. Seal this Ramadan series of therapy, which we pray Allah will accept from us all, with us understanding this point.

The simplest statements are the ones that will earn us the greatest rewards from Allah. The one *āyat* from the Qur'an, is the greatest *āyat* of the Qur'an, *Āyatul Kursi*. It protects us from harm. The last two verses from Surah al-Baqarah which were the chapters with which we began. Those are the *du'ā'* that we studied in the earlier chapters. Consider that the simplest of deeds will earn us the greatest of rewards and make this testament to it. May Allah make us worthy of our place with Him in a high standing in Jannah.

May Allah make our deeds testament for us that Allah will create for them love. May Allah create for us love in this life and give us His Greatest Love on the Day of Judgement and join us because of our love for Him, and our love for his Prophet s.a.w. in the highest levels of al-Firdaus, with and in the circles of the Prophets and the martyrs and the verifiers of truths and the righteous. *Allahumma āmīn*. May Allah s.w.t. elevate our names. May Allah s.w.t. make mention of us as we make mention of Him. May we remember Allah and make *du'ā'* to Allah outside the month of Ramadan as we have been persistent in it. May Allah give us the accomplishment of *taqwa* before the end of Ramadan. May Allah accept from us and our family our fast, our *qiyam, ruku'* and *sujud, Allahumma āmīn*. May Allah accept from all of us the blessings that we have sought to fulfil in our deeds and worship. May Allah s.w.t. return it upon us in greater and greater *barakah*. May Allah accept our charity in the little that we have offered towards others in service.

This is where, I, Yahya Ibrahim ask the readers in conclusion, to remember me, the weak brother, the sinful Yahya Ibrahim in your sincere *du'ā'*. May Allah grant me and my family *istiqamah* and firmness of heart upon faith and that of my children and our children's children, until all of us return to Allah. Anything that was good in this book, that was said, that was correct were from the blessings of Allah and the teachings of the Messenger Muhammad s.a.w. While anything of error, it is from me and from the influence of *shaytān* and Allah and His Messenger are free from blemish. *Jazakumullahukhair.*

Glossary

Adhān – Announcement; The Muslim call to Friday public worship (jumuʿah) and to the five daily hours of prayer

Adhkār – Plural of dhikr

Ākhirah – The Hereafter; the eternal spiritual realm

Al-Anbiya – The Prophets; plural of *nabi*

Aqidah – Creed

Dajjal – The false messiah, liar, the deceiver, the deceiving messiah

Daʿawāt – Invocations

Dhikr – Reminder; short phrases or prayers that are repeatedly recited silently within the mind or aloud to remember Allah

Duniya – The temporal world—and its earthly concerns and possessions

Fitnah – Temptation, trial; sedition, civil strife, conflict

Hadith – A collection of traditions containing sayings

of the Prophet Muhammad which, with accounts of his daily practice (the Sunnah), constitute the major source of guidance for Muslims apart from the Quran

Halal – Permissible; allowed

Haram – Forbidden

Hujjah – Proof; It is usually used to refer to a single individual in any given human era who represents God's "proof" to humanity.

Insha Allah – If Allah wills

Muadhin – the person who gives the call to prayer at a mosque

Riba' – usury, or unjust, exploitative gains made in trade or business under Islamic law

Ruqyah – the healing method based on the Quran and hadith through the recitation of the Quran, seeking of refuge, remembrance and supplication that is used as a means of treating sickness and other problems, by reading verses of the Quran, the names and attributes of Allah, or by using the prayers in Arabic or in a language, the meaning of which is understood

Sahābah – Companions of the Prophet

Salawat – Prayer or salutation upon Prophet Muhammad s.a.w.

Solatul Maghrib – one of the five mandatory salah (Islamic prayer). It is the fourth prayer of the day.

Sunnah – The body of traditional social and legal custom and practice of the Islamic community. Along with the Qur'ān (the holy book of Islam) and Hadith (recorded sayings of the Prophet Muhammad), it is a major source of Sharī'ah, or Islamic law.

Surah – A portion or a set of verses of the Quran

Tawbah – Repentance

Tawhid – The indivisible oneness concept of monotheism in Islam

Ulama' – The body of religious scholars who are versed theoretically and practically in the Muslim sciences

Wudū' – The Islamic procedure for cleansing parts of the body, a type of ritual purification, or ablution